PRAISE FOR
THE WEARY LEADER'S GUIDE ~~TO BURNOUT~~

The Weary Leader's Guide to Burnout is an exceptional book filled with helpful and thoughtful content. I'm so grateful for Sean Nemecek and the courage he shows in writing this book. I gladly commend it to folks.

—CHUCK DEGROAT, licensed therapist, spiritual director, and author of *When Narcissism Comes to Church*

Writing from the wisdom of painful experience and with broad expertise and deep compassion, Sean Nemecek has compiled a superior, comprehensive, and practical resource to help leaders recognize, treat, and even prevent the burnout that has become an epidemic in our time. Read and work through this book for the long-term health of your soul, your relationships, and your ministry. Your journey to full recovery begins with *The Weary Leader's Guide to Burnout*.

—ANGIE WARD, author of *Uncharted Leadership* and assistant director of the doctor of ministry program at Denver Seminary

The Weary Leader's Guide to Burnout is a hopeful and necessary gift to the legion of pastors who wonder how much longer they can continue. Author, pastor coach, and researcher Sean Nemecek guides us through his own journey while offering a path through the storm of burnout and ministry fatigue. The good news: burnout is not inevitable. The better news: there is great life after burnout. Sean's life is dedicated to serving pastors, and in this book you'll find an empathic and skilled guide for your own pastoral journey.

—STEVE CUSS, speaker and author of *Managing Leadership Anxiety*

The Weary Leader's Guide to Burnout is essential reading not only for those who are experiencing exhaustion but for all who have been called to ministry leadership. Sean Nemecek writes with the practical and compassionate wisdom of lived experience, offering theological and psychological insights, compelling stories, and spiritual practices that help us cooperate with the Holy Spirit for transformation and freedom. Through probing diagnostic questions that encourage deep reflection, Sean holds up mirrors so we can see our compulsions and captivities, and with that healed vision, see more clearly the invitations from Jesus to rest in his love and yield to his grace. I hope this outstanding soul-care book will not only be on leaders' desks but on seminary syllabi everywhere.

—SHARON GARLOUGH BROWN, spiritual director and author
of the Sensible Shoes series and Shades of Light series

The Weary Leader's Guide to Burnout is absolutely packed with great material. I found myself saying "yes" so many times. This book will be a great help to pastors.

—CHARLES STONE, author of *People-Pleasing Pastors*

I know scores of pastors and leaders who are overworked and overlooked. For those who are ministering within the institutional church, *The Weary Leader's Guide to Burnout* might be the practical permission slip you need to shift into a rhythm of life and work that doesn't crush your soul.

—K J. RAMSEY, therapist and author of *The Book of
Common Courage* and *The Lord Is My Courage*

Pastors are facing an epidemic of burnout. If, like me, you've experienced it, you know how debilitating it can be. In *The Weary Leader's Guide to Burnout*, Sean Nemecek offers practical, clinical, and biblical solutions to what we're facing. I highly recommend this book if you're experiencing the symptoms of burnout—or, better yet, before you get there.

—KARL VATERS, pastor and author of *The Grasshopper
Myth* and *Small Church Essentials*

Reading Sean's book is like visiting with a friend who knows what your soul really needs. He offers practical and experienced help that is vital for recovering from burnout as he shares from his own story and the stories of others. If you are experiencing burnout, think you might be heading in that direction, or know someone who is, this book is a gift—a wise guide that many will be using for a long time.

—KAYLENE DERKSEN, president of the Soul Care Institute

Sean has known the impact of burnout firsthand, and *The Weary Leaders Guide to Burnout* is a robust exploration of the nature and causes of burnout—told with both technical precision and personal transparency. Taking cues from his own journey, Sean has captured the heart of the gospel and brought it to bear in practical ways on both *recovering* from burnout and *creating* a ministry lifestyle that is resilient. Each chapter refuses to let the needy reader escape with just more information. Through insightful questions we are invited to think clearly about our current path toward health or burnout. These pages reveal a path for every weary leader to find new hope and a new way to live and serve. I am both grateful and proud that Sean is part of the PIR Ministries team. This book will become central in our toolkit of helping ministry leaders deal with burnout, and I would strongly recommend it as required reading for every ministry leader.

—ROY A. YANKE, executive director of PIR Ministries

A Journey from Exhaustion to Wholeness

THE
WEARY
LEADER'S
GUIDE TO
BURNOUT

SEAN NEMECEK

ZONDERVAN
REFLECTIVE

ZONDERVAN REFLECTIVE

The Weary Leader's Guide to Burnout
Copyright © 2023 by Sean Nemecek

Requests for information should be addressed to:
Zondervan, *3900 Sparks Dr. SE, Grand Rapids, Michigan 49546*

Zondervan titles may be purchased in bulk for educational, business, fundraising, or sales promotional use. For information, please email SpecialMarkets@Zondervan.com.

ISBN 978-0-310-14452-6 (audio)

Library of Congress Cataloging-in-Publication Data

Names: Nemecek, Sean, author.
Title: The weary leader's guide to burnout : a journey from exhaustion to wholeness / Sean
    Nemecek.
Description: Grand Rapids : Zondervan, 2023.
Identifiers: LCCN 2022047797 (print) | LCCN 2022047798 (ebook) | ISBN 9780310144502
    (paperback) | ISBN 9780310144519 (ebook)
Subjects: LCSH: Christian leadership. | Burn out (Psychology)--Religious aspects--Christianity. |
    BISAC: RELIGION / Christian Ministry / Pastoral Resources | RELIGION / Leadership
Classification: LCC BV652.1 .N396 2023 (print) | LCC BV652.1 (ebook) | DDC 262/.1--dc23/
    eng/20221129
LC record available at https://lccn.loc.gov/2022047797
LC ebook record available at https://lccn.loc.gov/2022047798

Cover design: Darren Welch Design
Cover art: © Khoj_Badami / Getty Images
Book diagrams: Paxcurio Studio, paxcuriostudio.com
Interior design: Sara Colley

Printed in the United States of America

23 24 25 26 27 28 29 30 31 32   /TRM/   13 12 11 10 9 8 7 6 5 4 3 2 1

CONTENTS

Foreword by Glenn Packiam ix

Introduction xiii

PART 1: UNDERSTANDING BURNOUT

1. Am I in Burnout? 3
2. Many Paths to Burnout 18
3. The Inner Life 31
4. Stress and Burnout 45
5. Energy and Rhythms 61

PART 2: RECOVERING FROM BURNOUT

6. Reconnecting 77
7. Restoration of Self 91
8. Becoming Secure 105
9. Differentiation of Self 120
10. Soul Care 133
11. Boundaries 144
12. Breaking Free 160

PART 3: RESILIENCE AGAINST BURNOUT

13. Never Burn Out Again 179
14. Surrender to God 193
15. Loving Life. 204
16. Beyond Burnout 214

Appendix 1: Planning Your Sabbath 227
Appendix 2: How to Create a Rule of Life 233
Acknowledgments 239
Notes 243

FOREWORD

A couple years ago, I read about the late chief rabbi of the British Commonwealth Lord Rabbi Jonathan Sacks getting his first stress test. When the doctor strapped the sensors on him and instructed him to get on the treadmill and run, the rabbi wondered why. "Are you testing how far I can run?" he wondered. "Or perhaps how fast I can run?" After he was done and finally caught his breath, he asked what on earth the doctor was testing. "How quickly you recover," the doctor replied. Recovery is an essential part of health.

We tend to think that being healthy means never getting sick or never experiencing stress. If we were healthier—in our minds, bodies, and emotions and in our relationship with God—then surely we would be unwavering, unshaken. But this is not true. Health is not merely about being well; it's also about getting well. Recovery is a marker of health.

It's no secret that pastoral work has become increasingly more challenging recently. As I have talked with hundreds of pastors over the past couple years for the Resilient Pastor initiatives, I have heard them say over and over again how unusual this moment of ministry is.

Yes, the world is changing, but it isn't just cultural tides and shifting attitudes. It's also the accumulating expectations of what a pastor should be. Decades ago, it may have been that a pastor was seen as a holy person, a sort of God-expert or Bible-answer guru. Later, pastors were asked to learn the newest insights from the world of therapy. They were expected to be skilled counselors, keen guides for the soul, or relationship experts for husbands and wives and parents. Then came a wave of church-planting, uber-successful CEO-pastors. Many pastors were measured against entrepreneurs and innovators and expected to be brilliant organizational leaders. Shortly after that, pastors were told they needed to be political commentators or social activists, keenly aware of each cultural issue and how to address it with wisdom and timeliness.

The mere shifting of expectations every few years alone would be too much. But these expectations haven't merely shifted; they've *stacked*. Pastors are supposed to be all these things at once. In the kaleidoscope of expectations projected on us from congregations, pastors are the ones whose lives gets contorted and stretched. These stacking expectations are compounded by the new digital world where everyone posts clips and content from church, and pastors and churches are being compared to each other like mannequins in the window.

It's no wonder that when Barna asked pastors if they had seriously considered quitting vocational ministry, the percentage who said yes rose from 29 percent in January of 2021 to 38 percent in October of 2021 to 43 percent in April of 2022. The job is becoming more complex.

Yet our calling to be faithful shepherds has never been more urgent. A darkening world needs pastors who can help form a community in Jesus's name and who will walk in Jesus's way as a witness in the world of the good news that Jesus is King. We need more pastors, not fewer. And we need pastors who will last.

What Sean has given us in this book is one of the most valuable resources for pastors. It is one part a diagnostic tool, one part medicine, and one part inoculation. Drawing on experience, psychology, and theology, it will help you uncover the root causes of burnout, map out a plan for recovery, and cultivate resilience so you never burn out again.

Best of all, Sean writes not only with wisdom and insight but with empathy. He has burned out—three times and in three different degrees of burnout. He knows the pain, the despair, the anger, and the hurt. He writes as "a wounded healer," to borrow Nouwen's phrase.

Jesus said that in this world we will have trouble. We will never eliminate the challenges of ministry in a fallen world. But Jesus said we can take heart because he has overcome the world. The righteous are compared to trees. When they are rooted, trees may sway and bend, but they will not break or fall. Recovery and resilience are what we need now more than ever, and this book will help the weary, the wounded, and the worn-out find both.

GLENN PACKIAM

Lead Pastor, Rockharbor Church

Author, *The Resilient Pastor, The Intentional Year*

INTRODUCTION

Amy and I lay in bed listening to the early morning rain through the open window. The sounds of large raindrops falling through the trees and gentle, distant thunder rolling across the rural landscape were just enough to keep us awake. As the heart of the storm drew closer and the thunder became louder, we could feel the tension in the air. Suddenly, the room lit up and the loudest boom I've ever heard shook the house—light and sound were practically simultaneous. I could tell the lightning had struck within a couple hundred yards of our house. Now we were fully awake!

"I hope our neighbors are okay," I half chuckled as I tried to calm my nerves and slow my heart rate. The Stagg family lived next door in a house set back from the road and up on a hill even with the back of our three-acre property. Between our house and theirs was a wooded rise, and I judged the lightning had probably struck the large maple that stood opposite Tom and Heather's house.

The storm diminished, and we were just dozing back off when we heard Heather's voice outside our bedroom window shouting, "Call 9-1-1! Our house is on fire!" even as Tom came running up our basement stairs and began knocking on the door for help. The lightning had, in fact, struck their house and started a small fire in the attic. They could see wisps of smoke leaking out the soffit. Amy dialed the emergency number as I let the Staggs into our home. It didn't take long before dense smoke rolled down the hill and settled in the valley around our house. I can still remember the acrid smell.

When the firefighters finished their work, soot stains on the siding and a hole in the roof marked the only external evidence of a fire. But internally, the fire had spread throughout the attic and weakened the structure of the house. Now the whole roof needed to be replaced.

Several days later, as the builders began the work of restoration, they started by removing the roof to prepare for the rebuild. That very evening it rained again—harder than I've ever seen—and drenched the inside of the house. A waterfall of rain gushed down the stairs of our friends' home, damaging every level of the house.

Over the next year, the Staggs endured great difficulty in working to restore their house. The water had damaged many of their possessions, and in the weeks it took to clear their possessions out, mold settled on everything else. Every item they owned had to be sent away for professional cleaning or be replaced. The house was gutted right down to the studs. The roof was rebuilt, and all the carpet, plaster, trim, and most of the electrical wiring was ripped out, filling dumpster after dumpster with rotting building materials. Then they refilled the house with industrial dehumidifiers and fans for the weeks-long drying process.

Rebuilding began several months after the fire. The builders replaced damaged wood, installed new wiring, cleaned the air ventilation, and laid new flooring through the house. In the end, the Staggs' house was rebuilt to better than before.

The trauma of that morning is still vivid, but God loved and cared for our friends through the whole ordeal. It's amazing how he can use life's worst events to show us his love and bless us so that we are better than we were before.

BURNOUT

My experience of burnout felt very much like our neighbors' house fire. I was scorched, damaged, and empty. The condition of my soul worsened before it got better, but that's the way of healing: Demolition comes before rebuilding. Some leaders need a sufficient amount of pain to wake them up to their need for change. I had to be broken before I could see my need for healing. Through the hard work of recovery and spiritual transformation, I became much better than I was before. God was working through the pain.

Years later, I still don't know how to tell my story of burnout without sounding angry or bitter toward some of the people involved. In my heart, I no longer feel that way toward them. But reliving the trauma, criticism, and grief brings back painful memories. Telling my story honestly means expressing those emotions. My intent is not to portray people I genuinely love as bad or hurtful. They were doing the best they could at the time, and I had some serious problems of my own. Dealing with a burned-out shell of a pastor must have been difficult.

My burnout came from years of unresolved conflict, what felt like constant criticism, and frustration over unrealized expectations and dreams. Two years into ministry, we experienced major church conflict that seemed like it would cause the end of my ministry. Even when that died down, significant personal and relational issues in my private life drove me toward my first instance of low-grade burnout. All the while, criticism continued from a small contingent of people at the church. On top of that, several people in our congregation died over a short period of time. I had been at the church long enough that the people we were burying were not just church acquaintances—they were my friends.

Then during a counseling session with a young man from the church, he got a call that his sister had been in an accident. I rushed him to the hospital to be with his family. When we arrived, we learned that his sister had died. Walking with this family through their grief, I felt something snap in my soul. "Lord, I can't take any more death right now," I prayed. This was my second experience of low-grade burnout. I never fully recovered from it. I made a few changes and improved for a little while, but I was already on a long, slow slide into deep burnout.

Physically, my body was just as unwell as my soul. I wasn't sleeping. I felt constant nagging pain in my shoulders and back. I started having cluster headaches and migraines far worse than I had ever experienced. I even had panic attacks. Those were particularly scary because I'm not usually prone to panic; in fact, I tend to become calmer and more clearheaded in stressful situations. By the time I realized I was in burnout, I was showing symptoms of posttraumatic stress, chronic traumatic stress, and compassion fatigue.

I continued in ministry, but my soul felt empty. I no longer recognized myself. The only parts of me that remained were my love for my family, my faith in God, and my sense of call to the ministry— although I increasingly questioned that.

During the most intense period of burnout, one of my critics brought up something from nine years earlier in an attempt to get me fired. For the first two years of my ministry, he had looked for every opportunity to criticize me to one of the board members. I found out years later that he had voted against me when the church called me to be their pastor. His constant resistance and complaining created a small but vocal dissenting group within the congregation. I attempted to reconcile with him, but he showed no interest. So I suggested he might be happier in another church. Now, almost a decade later, he brought this to our church's board, hoping it would end my ministry there. The board's enquiry into the event felt like an inquisition, and I feared losing my job. Because of the housing market crash, we wouldn't be able to sell our house for what we owed on it. I was terrified.

In one particularly confrontational meeting, my church board accused me of being lazy. I knew I was working hard, but because of my burnout, I was ineffective. They were right to question me. I should have confessed my struggles at that time, but I did not yet understand what was happening. I don't remember what I said, but I lashed back with accusations and hurtful words. As I said these things, I remember thinking, "Why are you saying that? That's not like you!"

The amygdala, the fear center of my brain, was in control. My brain perceived that I was in trouble and responded to protect me before I was consciously aware of what was happening. It was like having an out-of-body experience. I didn't recognize myself. I was like a volcano spewing out the lava that had accumulated in my soul. I responded to pain by causing pain. That shocked me because I'm usually a kind and gentle person.

After a long enquiry and a face-to-face meeting between me, my critic, and two members of the board, my name was cleared. My critic had made wild accusations without any evidence. It was his word against mine. By the grace of God, I remained calm and caring in the face of his anger. The board couldn't find any evidence of wrongdoing (though as I look back, I should have handled many things differently). My critic left the church to attend another one, where he was much happier. Immediately, the conflict dissipated, and I was free to focus on my work.

As the dust settled, I began to search for answers. My soul's eruption during that confrontation made me keenly aware something was wrong deep inside. I realized this had been my third experience of burnout. The first two times, I knew I was exhausted by conflict, grief, and frustration, but I didn't recognize I was in low-grade burnout. I got some rest and made some changes, but those things didn't lead to full recovery. This time, I barely survived. I knew that if something didn't change, my next experience would kill me. I would have a heart attack, commit suicide, or throw my life away in some other way.

I'm wired in such a way that when I have something to learn, I don't do it halfway. I'm like a rottweiler with a bone: nothing will stop me until I have the answers I seek. Sometimes this drive becomes all-consuming and unhealthy, but at this point in my life, I was like a man in the desert desperately searching for life-giving water. Over the next few years, I read books on counseling, leadership, soul care, and trauma—anything I could find to heal my soul. I secured the help of a professional Christian counselor, a spiritual director, a ministry coach, and a mentor. I began meeting regularly with a close friend who enjoyed being with me and had no interest in changing me. I talked to my doctor about my physical symptoms. He advised me to reduce my stress load by taking as much time off as I could. Each of these people helped me step out of the darkness of isolation and into the light of healthy community.

Slowly, I healed and found a new way to live. Some changes came quickly, but my full healing has been a years-long journey—one that may continue the rest of my life. Along the way I met God again, and he introduced me to myself (in some ways for the first time). I learned the importance of rest, but until I also learned how to transform my pain into strength, that knowledge didn't do me any good. That's what this book is about: the practical, spiritual, and personal movements that lead us from burnout to healing and from healing to thriving. It's about relationships with God, others, and self that help us become better after we're broken.

BETTER AFTER BROKEN

This book is a practical resource to help you identify whether you're experiencing or approaching burnout, guide you through it, and teach you to establish practices that will build resilience for the future. The principles it contains are based on my own experience and the lessons I've learned from coaching burned-out leaders. Each part of the book represents a different movement from understanding to behavior change to transformation. Part 1 explores what burnout is, what causes it, and mistakes leaders make that contribute to burnout. Part 2 provides the tools I used to climb out of burnout and into recovery. Some of these tools are time-tested; others I have developed and refined in my coaching work. We will focus on life-changing activities, behaviors, and practices that might help you climb out too. In part 3 I will lead you on a spiritual journey of transformation, guiding you from the dead end of burnout down the narrow way of Christ. This is where you will learn to thrive and maybe even become burnout-proof.

Based on my experience as a pastor and my work of coaching pastors, I've written this book with Christian leaders in mind.[1] Think of me as a guide who has walked this path ahead of you. I'm here to point out the landmarks and pitfalls on your road to recovery and transformation. However, you are the expert on you. Only you can probe the depths of your own burnout. Therefore, *the results will be up to you.* The value you get from this book will depend on the effort you put into it. Be patient with God and with yourself. Recovering from burnout is hard work. With coaching, most people experience significant change in three to six months. However, based on my experience, I know that healing can take three to five years. So take your time. This is not a book to speed read; it contains a lot of information, and if you read too quickly, you may feel overwhelmed. Try to read slowly, and take time to thoughtfully engage the reflection questions in each chapter.

Unfortunately, some people choose to remain stuck. They may change jobs or find new leadership positions, but their cycle of burnout will follow them wherever they go. Others will walk only partway down the path; they will find some tools to recover but won't do the hard work of transformation. Becoming whole requires deep sacrifice, and they may decide the cost is too high. These leaders will probably experience burnout again and again. And that's okay.

Like me, when they are ready, they will return to this path, and God will lead them to health. My prayer is that you will look fear in the face, count the cost, and push through—until you experience transformation into a new way of being with God and others.

I hope you will do the hard work, but please understand that only God can bring about full transformation. Like all movements of grace, it's God's work not ours. Our job is to show up and be attentive to God and open to his transforming work. You may feel broken now, but that's where God does his best work. When he's done, you will be a healthier and more authentic you. You will be better after broken.

PART 1

UNDERSTANDING BURNOUT

1

AM I IN BURNOUT?

The local landfill in Centralia, Pennsylvania, had become a major problem. People living nearby complained about the smell and how papers carried by the wind from the landfill littered the town. Although you won't find it in the meeting minutes, Centralia's city council decided to clean up the dump by setting it on fire. Burning landfills was prohibited by state law, but on May 27, 1962, someone struck a match.

The council intended the fire to burn for only one day to get rid of the smell and the litter. According to David Dekok's book *Fire Underground*, they even hired five firefighters (again, off the books) to extinguish the flames at the end of the day.[1] But after the controlled burn was finished and everyone had left, somewhere in the middle of all that rubbish, embers continued to glow.

Two days later, the caretaker at the local cemetery noticed the smoke. When he went to check it out, he saw the small landfill ablaze. Though some people deny it, experts believe the landfill fire ignited a vein of anthracite coal in the Centralia mine. Even after sixty years, this fire is still raging today.

Burning at a depth of 300 feet, the eight-mile-long Centralia mine fire is barely noticeable most of the time. However, it occasionally creeps toward the surface, creating unstable ground that cracks roads, forms sink holes, and vents toxic carbon monoxide into the air. Portions of the ground under the village of Centralia have registered temperatures exceeding 900 degrees. The city had to be abandoned.

Some fires burn hot and bright, like the wildfires that occasionally sweep through the western United States. They are visible for miles, and crews come from all over to help contain and extinguish the blaze. Other fires smolder below the surface, unseen but spreading and destroying from within. Leadership burnout is usually a slow fire smoldering deep beneath the surface, consuming the fuel leaders need to thrive, leaving them empty.

Most leaders are unaware when they are burning out. Cracks begin to develop on the surface of their lives, but they are quick to dismiss them as a little stress or an unusually busy season. They may begin to blame others for their working conditions or their problems at home. What they don't realize is that they have an inferno deep within their soul that's becoming toxic and will soon cause catastrophic damage in their lives. It could happen at any moment, and they are completely oblivious.

In this chapter, I want to share with you what burnout looks like externally and how it feels internally. Based on my personal experience, the work I do coaching, and leading workshops for burned-out leaders, I'll profile the types of leaders who are likely to burn out and answer the question, "How can I know if I'm in burnout?"

Whenever I share my story of burnout with others, something in it connects with their stress, fatigue, or anxiety. When they ask, "Am I burning out?" I know I'm probably talking to a leader. They may not be a CEO or a pastor, but they probably hold some kind of leadership responsibility. Parents, teachers, therapists, managers, and other leaders see potential for positive change and call others toward growth. They don't just walk away when the plan isn't working. Often, they push and push until they feel stuck, tired, and hopeless. They struggle to find answers, wondering what is happening and why they've lost their creativity and drive.

WHAT IS BURNOUT?

The blaze in the Centralia mines continues to burn unseen. Even though the fires are monitored, no one knows how far they have spread or where they will surface next. In the same way, burnout can be difficult to define. It can show up in many ways, and each experience is unique. Perhaps that's why the *Diagnostic and Statistical Manual of Mental Disorders* (DSM-5) contains no definition or description of burnout. According to the Mayo Clinic, burnout is simply work-related stress, "a state of physical or emotional exhaustion that also involves a sense of reduced accomplishment and loss of personal identity."[2] The World Health Organization says that burnout is a syndrome that results from "chronic workplace stress that has not been successfully managed."[3] This definition highlights that burnout has to do with both our work culture and our internal response to that culture.

I believe that *burnout is what happens when our inner life with God is no longer able to sustain our outer work for God.* A misalignment between our inner life and our outer work leads to a hollowing of the soul as we expend more emotional and spiritual energy than we take in. Spiritual author Henri Nouwen, in describing his own burnout, said "I was living in a very dark place and the term 'burnout' was a convenient psychological translation for a spiritual death"[4] In part 2, we will explore how to bring both inner and outer life into alignment, and in part 3, I will show you a spiritual path that can transform you into a fireproof leader—one who may never burn out again.

Burnout is the condition of having your personal identity overwhelmed by the anxiety of life—a total depletion of self. It's like you have been separated from yourself in the smoke and fires of life. You keep looking for yourself, but it's too dark and you can't breathe. To survive, you eventually give up, stop looking for your true self, and become someone else. You abandon yourself to the smoke and fire and start to live a lie. When that lie catches up with you, you become alone, exhausted, and afraid. *Burnout is losing yourself in the fire.*

Diagnosing Burnout

To determine the way forward, we must first understand our current situation. Here are three diagnostic tools developed by mental health professionals to help people explore the scale and scope of their burnout.

The Maslach Burnout Inventory (MBI) measures a person's emotional exhaustion, cynicism, and professional efficacy, rating the person from low to high in each category. According to this widely used inventory, a person with high emotional exhaustion, high cynicism, and low professional efficacy is at a greater risk of experiencing burnout.

Unlike the Maslach Burnout Inventory, which was developed to assess professional burnout in human service, education, business, and government, the Francis Burnout Inventory (FBI) was created to assess clergy specifically. It measures how the negative aspects of your work are balanced out by the positive ones.[5] In other words, do you have enough positive emotional experiences in your work to help you overcome the negative emotional impacts?

The Areas of Worklife Survey (AWS) measures factors in your work environment or culture that may be contributing to burnout across six categories:

Workload: how much the demands of your work affect other
    areas of life
Control: how much autonomy you have in your work
Reward: how much recognition you receive for your job
Community: the health of the social context of your workplace
Fairness: how well everyone is treated with fairness and justice
Values: how what matters to you lines up with your
    organization[6]

Each of these diagnostic tools has a place in understanding the shape and depth of burnout. However, if you believe you're experiencing burnout, it's best not to rely only on your own interpretation of a diagnostic tool you found in a book or online. A qualified professional can help immensely with your self-reflection.

The Negative Impact of Burnout

A quick scan of the headlines reveals that burnout is costly to organizations. The toll it takes on churches, nonprofits, and other Christian organizations is substantial. Every year I talk with dozens of pastors who consider leaving their churches because of burnout. Not all of them end up leaving, but consider the costs involved with just one pastor leaving their church or one leader leaving their organization. The costs associated with turnover are more than just hiring a new leader. While that role is being filled, everyone in the organization has to make up for the gap. Productivity falls, communication gets messy, decision making becomes rushed, stress rises, and conflict becomes inevitable. Take out a key leader, and the whole organization suffers—whether it's management, employees and customers, or staff and congregation. No wonder Satan loves to target pastors.

On the individual level, burnout is associated with broken relationships, depression, addiction, and suicide. People who experience long-term burnout symptoms are more likely to report symptoms of posttraumatic stress, chronic stress, and the associated health conditions like heart and stomach ailments or disease. Burnout leads to impaired judgment, lack of focus, and difficulty remembering important tasks, responsibilities, or people. All of this can add up to diminished self-discipline leading to moral failure.

Helping workers fully recover from burnout if they've experienced it or become more resilient if they haven't yet are essential tasks for organizational health and the wellbeing of its workforce. I can tell you from personal experience and observing the lives of those I've coached through burnout that life is so much better when you have the tools to avoid burnout and enjoy fulfilling work.

What Does Burnout Look Like?

If you have to ask, "Am I in burnout?" the fire may already be smoldering deep in your soul. There are four indicators you can look for to know if you are in burnout: (1) deep fatigue, (2) diminished sense of accomplishment, (3) loss of self, and (4) hopelessness.[7] If it's truly burnout, all four indicators will be present.

The most basic sign of burnout is *deep fatigue*, a general tiredness that never goes away. Most burned-out leaders express emotional fatigue that impacts their physical energy. At first it may be a light surface-level feeling, like when you don't get enough sleep or you've had a long day at work. If left untreated, it will become a pervasive exhaustion that you can feel in your bones. That's how I felt. The depressive fatigue made it difficult to get out of bed in the morning, impossible to care for other people, and hard to do any work. Light exercise felt like a marathon. Basic self-care like showering, shaving, or brushing my teeth seemed herculean tasks. Everything in life felt heavier, like dragging an anchor through my day.

The second sign of burnout is a *diminished sense of accomplishment*. You may be doing the same work, but everything feels inexplicably harder. You just aren't getting the results you once did. Work that used to bring you joy now drains your soul. I loved being a pastor, and my work usually energized me, but in my state of burnout it left me feeling depleted, empty, and exhausted. I felt like a hamster on a wheel. No matter how hard I worked, I was stuck in the same place. Most burned out leaders will say things like, "I feel stuck, but I don't know why."

The third indicator is a *loss of self*. Feeling like a stranger in your own skin—a fraud, or an imposter—you find yourself questioning your calling. You no longer know what brings you joy. You no longer understand why you say the things you say or do the things you do. You doubt your strengths and magnify your weaknesses. You long for the days when you felt confident, self-assured, and capable. When I looked at myself in the mirror, it was like someone else's eyes were looking back at me. I wasn't experiencing God's love, and therefore I didn't feel secure in Christ. I struggled to read my Bible and pray. I felt like a failure instead of one who overwhelmingly conquers in Christ Jesus. I didn't understand why criticism hurt so much or why I quickly became defensive about everything. I couldn't even recognize my own feelings.

The final indicator in recognizing burnout is *hopelessness* or a loss of optimism. In addition to feeling stuck, burned-out leaders will feel imprisoned; they have no hope of escaping their despair. These leaders have lost the vision that used to propel them forward into the future. Now they don't believe there is a future for them. They are just waiting for someone to cast them aside. They've tried everything and nothing worked. I remember living in constant fear that I was going to lose my job, my house, and my reputation, and there was nothing I could do about it.

Here are the four questions you need to ask to know if you are in burnout:

1. Do you feel emotionally and physically fatigued?
2. Do you have a diminished sense of accomplishment?

3. Have you lost your sense of self?
4. Do you feel hopeless?

If your answer to all four questions is yes, then you are probably in burnout. In addition to these four signs, you may also be experiencing several issues that often accompany burnout.

You may be in *physical pain*. Headaches, muscle pain, or gastrointestinal problems can accompany the stress of burnout. I thought I was having a heart attack when my heart raced and felt like it was about to explode out of my chest. Now I know that feeling is really a panic attack. Minor skin problems, serious rashes, weight gain, toothaches, and many more physical symptoms may show up because your body is telling you that something is seriously wrong.

Burnout can also *intensify emotions*. Outbursts of anger, cynicism, or blame are normal responses to burnout. Sometimes a person just feels emotionally depleted or exhausted, like they no longer have the emotional resources to deal with everyday life. Things that previously were minor annoyances become major obstacles. For example, administrative duties that you were able to accomplish easily now leave you completely drained, angry, or confused. You may feel deeply depressed, like you could cry at any moment, without any explanation why. These emotions can become so strong that you start to block them out, leaving you numb and unable to feel anything.

Burnout can be accompanied by feelings of *guilt* or *shame*. Occasionally, burnout is caused by hiding from the real guilt of sin. Maintaining a lie or hiding a sin is stressful. If you live in constant fear that your sin will be uncovered, then you will eventually crash. You know that at some point "your sin will find you out" (Num. 32:23), and that knowledge will drive you beyond your limits. Guilt comes from doing things we know are wrong or from not doing things we know we are responsible for. We have a clear sense of why we feel guilty.

Shame shows up differently. Sometimes we have a vague feeling of guilt that we cannot place. Usually this is the false guilt known as shame. Feeling like you are less than others or that no one knows what you are going through can be indicators of shame.

Shame often manifests as negative self-talk. When you feel embarrassed, unsuccessful, or imperfect, what does your internal dialogue sound like? We all have negative internal critics, but when we are burning out, they become particularly nasty. We berate and abuse ourselves with insult and attack: "How could you be so stupid?" "You should know better!" "You're worthless." "No wonder no one loves you!" We would never talk to others this way, but for some reason we feel like we deserve the self-abuse. Burnout brought out the worst of my internal critic, and this negativity perpetuated the problem. I was circling downward in a shame spiral.

Sometimes that internal negativity is expressed in feelings of *hopelessness*, the sense that things will never get better. You feel trapped in a cave without any light and with no way forward. Things that once inspired you now leave you feeling discouraged. Optimistic or hopeful people begin to annoy you, and you're not sure why. You become like Eeyore from Winnie-the-Pooh, with a dark cloud hovering over any good news. You find yourself focusing on the negative and completely missing any good things that are happening. One pastor told me how he was discouraged by low worship attendance that week. When I asked him to tell me the good things that were happening in his church, he was shocked to remember that he had baptized thirty people just one week earlier!

The following chart contains several warning signs that you may be in burnout. Look it over and mark which ones resonate with you. The more of these you identify in yourself, the more likely you are burning out. Leaders (and their loved ones) should be continually watching for these signs that the stress has become too much for too long.

Warning Signs of Burnout

Internal Warning Signs	Physical Warning Signs
• Feeling depressed, angry, anxious, or on edge • Difficulty concentrating or feeling mentally tired • Negative view of self • Emotionally numb or bottled-up emotions • Feeling preoccupied, apathetic, or sad • No longer finding favorite activities pleasurable • Reoccurrence of nightmares or flashbacks to traumatic event • Hyper-arousal or hyper-vigilance (always on high alert for danger)	• Lethargy • Trouble sleeping • Chronic pain • Gastrointestinal problems • Low immunity • Back/neck pain • Headaches • Chronic fatigue syndrome • Fibromyalgia • High blood pressure • Weight gain/loss

WHAT BURNOUT ISN'T

Several stress responses may accompany and contribute to burnout but are not necessarily signs of burnout. They have different causes but similar symptoms. Some of these are very serious and may take years of specialized therapy to treat. If you think you have any one of these stress responses, please be sure to get help from a qualified professional.

Compassion Fatigue

Leaders in the caregiving fields (e.g., counselors, pastors, teachers, and social workers) can lose their ability to care for others. No matter how hard they try, they just can't seem to find compassion

Warning Signs of Burnout (continued)

Relational Warning Signs	*Behavioral Warning Signs*
• Withdrawal or isolation from others • Excessive or irrational blaming • Defensiveness or shame • Complaining a lot about administrative duties • Receiving an unusual number of complaints from others • Negative, pessimistic, or self-absorbed	• Poor self-care (e.g., hygiene, appearance, insomnia, overwork) • Compulsive behaviors (e.g., overspending, overeating, gambling, and other addictions) • Legal problems; debt • Substance abuse used to mask feelings • Difficulty doing normal activities

within themselves. When a leader gives more care than their internal life can sustain, mercy slowly turns to bitterness as they abuse their own body, mind, and spirit. They no longer find joy in helping people. Compassion fatigue is defined as "the physical and mental exhaustion and emotional withdrawal experienced by those who care for sick or traumatized people over an extended period of time" and "apathy or indifference toward the suffering of others as the result of overexposure to tragic news stories and images and the subsequent appeals for assistance."[8] Compassion fatigue is usually a sign that the leader does not have healthy rhythms of self-care. At this point, they themselves may need help from a mentor, spiritual director, or licensed counselor.

Compassion fatigue and burnout often appear simultaneously. One could argue that compassion fatigue is burnout for caregivers. However, in my experience compassion fatigue among Christian leaders usually happens before they are in full burnout. It may be a warning sign along the road, I've seen pastors struggling with compassion fatigue recover by taking a sabbatical or extended vacation and making a few simple changes to their life. The pastors I coach through burnout, take much longer to heal and require change at a much deeper level. For both burnout and compassion fatigue the attention of a therapist is usually helpful. However, therapy is essential to treat the following trauma responses.

Trauma Responses

There are three types of trauma responses that are occasionally confused with burnout: secondary trauma, posttraumatic stress, and complex traumatic stress. Each of these trauma responses may contribute to burnout, but they need to be treated separately by a qualified therapist. Trauma is connected to specific wounding events. They may be singular or recurring, but the hallmark of trauma is a physical or psychological wound. Pastor and burnout researcher Dr. Wes Beavis says:

> Burnout is not a sudden event. It doesn't jump out of nowhere to suddenly mug you and run off with your wellbeing. Rather, it has a stealth approach. It hacks into your wellbeing and steals small amounts over a long period of time. At first you may not notice the signs. But after a while, the compounding effect of micro-losses can bankrupt your spirit of vitality.[9]

So trauma is tied to specific events, but it's harder to identify the specific causes of burnout.

Secondary trauma (sometimes called vicarious trauma) comes from being exposed to trauma experienced by others. The *Psychiatric Times* describes secondary trauma as "indirect exposure to trauma through a firsthand account or narrative of a traumatic event."[10] Like compassion fatigue, secondary trauma is most common among leaders in the helping professions. Just by listening to someone relate a traumatic event, the helper becomes traumatized themselves. This type of stress should only be treated by a licensed professional counselor.

Posttraumatic stress (PTS or PTSD) is common among leaders in military, police, emergency, and health professions, but it can happen to anyone.[11] According to the National Center for PTSD, posttraumatic stress is "a mental health problem that some people develop after experiencing or witnessing a life-threatening event, like combat, a natural disaster, a car accident, or sexual assault."[12] PTS can come from being a victim or from being part of a traumatized group. In the United States, we have a long history of racialized trauma from the shame of race-based lending practices to the intense violence of lynching and shootings. Many rural communities have been traumatized by rampant drug addiction and suicide stemming from economic devastation. Even a family with a violent, alcoholic father could be considered a traumatized group. However, not all trauma happens in groups. It can even come from simply witnessing traumatic events like a car crash or terrorist attack on television. This type of stress also requires the expertise of a licensed professional counselor.

The symptoms of complex (or chronic) traumatic stress (CTS) look similar to PTS, but the source of the trauma isn't a single event. It's a mental health problem that develops when a person feels they cannot escape a situation in which they've experienced prolonged, repeated interpersonal trauma (either physical or emotional). "The wounds of complex trauma survivors are often so deep that their ability to live out of who God created them to be has been severely hampered," says Christian counselor Heather Gingrich.[13] Leaders who have a constant critic or who face continual conflict often develop CTS. Again, this traumatic stress should be treated under the supervision of a licensed professional counselor.

Are you seeing a theme? It's wise for every leader to check in with a licensed professional counselor on a yearly basis. Think of it like an annual wellness check, similar to what you might experience with your dentist or physician. If you find yourself in one of these chronic stress conditions, having a counselor you trust will be a great asset in helping you diagnose and treat the problem.

Emotional Exhaustion

Not everyone who experiences deep emotional exhaustion will fall into burnout. Some people have enough positive emotional experiences in their work to keep them going through the fatigue. Others have a support network that sustains them and gives them an outlet for expressing their pain or a place to find enough rest to keep going. These things keep the emotional exhaustion from progressing into deeper issues. According to Dr. Wes Beavis, emotional exhaustion is merely the first symptom of the stages of burnout. There's still time to turn things around before burning out.[14]

HOW HEALTHY ARE YOU?

Reflect on what we've covered so far. Just reading the words on the page won't help you identify your burnout. Reflect deeply and ask yourself some hard questions. Only through this type of interior work can you get a handle on what is really happening inside you. By mapping your interior life, you may be able to figure out where you lost yourself in the smoke and fire and what is draining all your resources. Take some time and evaluate your health and wellness in relation to your work and service. Here are a few questions to get you started:

1. What is happening in your life that led you to purchase this book?
2. As you were reading this chapter, which symptoms of burnout resonated with you? Why?
3. Look through the chart "Warning Signs of Burnout" earlier in this chapter. Which warning signs do you see in yourself?
4. Answer the four diagnostic questions from the section "What Does Burnout Look Like?" How strongly did you answer each one?

5. If you are in burnout, can you identify when it began? Create a timeline of your burnout. Include significant events or factors that contributed to your symptoms.

6. If you are not in burnout, what significant lessons did you learn from this chapter that will help you become resilient to burnout?

2

MANY PATHS TO BURNOUT

When I started telling others about my own burnout, they repeatedly responded, "You love your job, you're driven by passion, and you seem to have it all together. You're the last person I would expect to burn out." No one—especially me—thought burnout would happen to me. I was wrong.

But burnout isn't completely unpredictable. While it can happen to anyone, certain types of leaders are more likely to burn out, and unfortunately, the same things that make us good leaders can also lead to burnout. The qualities we might expect to prevent burnout often make us more susceptible.

In working with burned-out leaders, I have discovered several profiles that make them more likely to burn out. The following thirteen profiles paint a picture of the danger areas that all leaders face. They do not guarantee that such a leader will burn out, but leaders who fit these patterns are more likely to burn out because of their disordered lives and work culture. The examples provided with each profile are intended to illustrate the disorder, not necessarily portray a burned-out leader. I've broken them into three larger categories:

work dysfunction, *relational challenges*, and *self-sabotage*. I can see myself in many of these thirteen profiles. If you're not sure whether you are likely to experience burnout (or are already on that path), look for aspects of yourself in each one.

WORK DYSFUNCTION

The first four leadership profiles have to do with disordered relationships with work or dysfunctional workplaces. These leaders burn out because of what is or isn't happening in the workplace. Consider how your workplace culture could contribute to your burnout.

The Overworked Leader

If I were to ask, "Who is most likely to burn out?" you would probably say the *overworked leader*. It just seems logical—the longer and more often a candle is lit, the faster it will shrink into nothing. Often, leaders like this love their job or get lost in their work. A dysfunctional work culture either drives their overwork or allows them to hide from their problems in their work. This leader may not be able to keep up with all the work they are driven to do.

Some overworked leaders use work to avoid facing problems at home or within themselves. They haven't established boundaries around work because they don't want to take responsibility for themselves or their families. Lack of boundaries at work gives them an excuse to avoid this responsibility. This type of overwork may be driven by shame or family conflict. Eventually, hiding from their problems won't work anymore, and the internal or family problems start following them into the office. Overworking leaders sometimes endure horrible working conditions, deceit, and betrayal just to maintain their position within the company or church. With nowhere to hide from the problem, the overworked leader crashes, sometimes in dramatic and harmful ways. In Numbers 11:11–15, Moses experiences this type of overwhelming burden:

> He asked the LORD, "Why have you brought this trouble on your servant? What have I done to displease you that you put the burden of all these people on me? Did I conceive all these people? Did I give them birth? Why do you tell me to carry them in my arms, as a nurse carries an infant, to the land you promised on oath to their ancestors? Where can I get meat for all these people? They keep wailing to me, 'Give us meat to eat!' I cannot carry all these people by myself; the burden is too heavy for me. If this is how you are going to treat me, please go ahead and kill me—if I have found favor in your eyes—and do not let me face my own ruin."

Moses literally asks God to kill him because he cannot keep up with the work of caring for the people. Moses's death wish is a classic sign of an overworked leader.

The Underworking Leader

An underworking leader's lack of productivity leads to anxiety, which is a primary factor in burnout. This leader may be lazy or intentionally underworking because of personal or cultural problems within their workplace—doing only the bare minimum to keep their position of influence. This means that those under them must do more than their fair share of the work. Rather than empowering people, this leader uses people to prop up their leadership facade. How does underworking lead to burnout? Eventually this leader's resistance to their work will lead to conflict, which will reveal their poor performance. Most leaders intuitively know this and remaining in an underworking posture produces anxiety and shame that lead to burnout.

The Old Testament priest Eli is an example of a lazy leader. When Hannah was praying in deep anguish, Eli was watching her from a chair by the doorpost to the Lord's house. He didn't inquire to see what she was praying; he just assumed she was drunk and told her to stop drinking (1 Sam. 1:12–14). Eli's sons are described as thieving scoundrels in 1 Samuel 2:12–17. Eli rebuked his sons for their wickedness but didn't discipline them. God sent a prophet to Eli to rebuke him. Speaking for God, the prophet asked, "Why do you honor your sons more than me by fattening yourselves on the choice parts of every offering made by the people of Israel?" (1 Sam. 2:29). Therefore, because of his unfaithfulness as high priest, God rejected his whole household as priests over Israel. After the Philistines defeated the Israelites in battle, a messenger came to tell Eli that his sons had been killed and the ark of the covenant had been captured. "When he mentioned the ark of God, Eli fell backward off his chair by the side of the gate. His neck was broken and he died, for he was an old man, and he was heavy" (1 Sam. 4:18). Eli was a victim of his own laziness.

The Underutilized Leader

Another type of underworking leader is the underutilized leader. These leaders work hard but are frustrated because they have more to offer than is being asked of them. They may be overlooked in their areas of strength, feel their ideas are not valued, or believe they are being held down by a controlling supervisor. This lack of freedom and the accompanying frustration lead to dissatisfaction in their work. Staying in a place where one feels unfulfilled is a recipe for burnout.

I know of a youth pastor, Davis, who was in his early forties. He loved the work and was very good at it. Teens flocked to the church specifically to hear his teaching because he was an excellent leader who modeled the love of Jesus. Then the church hired a younger, insecure senior pastor. This new pastor micromanaged Davis and limited his authority. He was no longer free to lead as he was able but had to get permission for everything. Frustrated and tired of fighting with his inexperienced leader, Davis left youth ministry for a marketplace job.

The Misaligned Leader

Misaligned leaders work outside their area of strength or in a work culture that doesn't fit their values. These leaders get things done, but because they are working in areas that do not motivate them or where they don't have a natural ability, everything takes more effort and energy. Their work drains their mental and emotional reserves. If these leaders don't have an external source of renewal, they will soon run out of energy.

I was a city boy in a rural church. As a visionary leader and early adopter of change, the cultural preference for status quo and resistance to change created much of the conflict I endured. I could never wrap my mind around why rural cultures would rather die than change, and that meant that I would never be truly accepted in that community. I was always an outsider in a culture that didn't trust outsiders. It wasn't until I took an assessment called the PRO-D[1] that I realized I was never going to be able to fit within the culture of the church. Now, as a PRO-D facilitator, I help other pastors avoid or understand this mistake.

The Underappreciated Leader

Like an underutilized leader, underappreciated leaders may feel like they are being overlooked. They rarely hear the encouragement they need to thrive and might be working in highly critical workplaces where their faults are always on display. It is possible that they are excellent leaders who get the job done and empower people, but no one acknowledges their ability. They may be good leaders whom people love to follow, but they work under perfectionistic supervisors who push them to eliminate their weaknesses while never valuing their strengths. A true leader learns to accept their weaknesses and maximize their strengths. But underappreciated leaders can feel trapped by their weaknesses instead of freed to follow their strengths. Feeling trapped is an early sign that burnout may be around the corner.

Maria is an imaginative and capable leader in a male-dominated work culture. Because she is a woman, she is not allowed to hold authoritative roles. The man she works under continually implements her ideas because he has the authority to do so. When he is praised for Maria's ideas, he doesn't share the spotlight. This kind of unjust underappreciation happens to women in many workplaces. Can you see how this would rightly lead to anger, frustration, anxiety, and shame? Maria left her job and found one where she would be valued, and now she is thriving.

RELATIONAL CHALLENGES

The next four leadership types burn out because of a lack of quality, encouraging, or safe relationships. They may lack friends, be in conflict, or have a dysfunctional home life. Whatever the cause, these leaders need good friends and teammates to help them thrive.

The Isolated Leader

If I had to pick one profile most likely to burn out, it would be the isolated leader. These are men and women who have become disconnected from friends, family, and other support networks. They don't have anyone to ask them the hard questions or keep them accountable. They may have chosen to self-isolate as a way of avoiding their problems, or they may not have anyone nearby who understands their struggles. Many pastors are terribly isolated. Because of their role, it can be hard for them to find safe people in their own churches, and other pastors in their communities often see them as the competition rather than as a partner in ministry. Leadership, by nature, can be isolating, and it's up to the leader to find ways to keep this from happening. When leaders don't find connection and support, they will eventually burn out.

Elijah in 1 Kings 19 is a prime example of an isolated leader. He singlehandedly represented God by facing down 850 prophets of Baal and Asherah on Mount Carmel. God did the miracle, but Elijah stood alone. So when Jezebel sought to avenge the death of her prophets, Elijah fled to the wilderness, where he sat down under a broom tree and waited to die. Elijah sleeping under a broom tree is the perfect picture of what it's like to be an isolated, burned-out leader. God sent an angel to feed and care for Elijah before calling him to Mount Horeb. There on the mountain, Elijah confessed his frustrations "I have been very zealous for the LORD God Almighty. The Israelites have rejected your covenant, torn down your altars, and put your prophets to death with the sword. I am the only one left, and now they are trying to kill me too" (v. 10). Do you hear the exhaustion, isolation, loss of call, and hopelessness in Elijah's complaint? Ged then pointed out that Elijah wasn't alone and that he had preserved 7,000 people in Israel. To combat Elijah's isolation, God appointed Elisha who would be Elijah's partner and successor. Isolated leaders often burn out because they don't see anyone to share the load.

The Conflicted Leader

Conflicted leaders live with constant relational anxiety—the internal fire that leads to burnout. These leaders may stir up conflict everywhere they go because of shame, low self-esteem, or a narcissistic personality. Or they may avoid conflict and therefore never resolve anything. Neither type of leader resolves conflict, so both are plagued by it. They lack the skills to work through conflict and find unity. Living in constant conflict leaves them feeling like hollowed out shells.

King Saul was a man of constant conflict. He lacked the humility to do the things that would lead to peace. He fought against Samuel, David, and even God—who all would have been on his side if he had let them join him. Instead, Saul blamed everyone else for his problems, which meant he could never find peace within. When David fought for Saul and gained victory for Israel, Saul became jealous. He was convinced that David was out to take his throne even though David had refused to do so on several occasions. Saul was so given over to delusion that he even attacked his own son Jonathan for declaring that David was innocent (1 Sam. 20). The conflict within Saul led him to distrust his most loyal friends and eventually led to his downfall.

The Traumatized Leader

The third type of relationally challenged leader is one who has been traumatized or abused. These leaders may be unable to trust others or connect with them on a deeper level. Keeping everyone at a safe distance is a defensive tactic that may have served them well in the past. However, it will make everything harder in their current leadership role. People follow leaders they trust, and trust is built on personal connection. A traumatized leader who hasn't found healing from the trauma or abuse will have to work harder to lead people from a distance. Eventually, their best people will go where they feel trusted. To recover from burnout, these leaders will need to learn to trust others and lean on them for help.

The story of Gideon in Judges 6–8 starts with the Israelites returning to their evil ways. So God allowed Midian to oppress them. The Midianites camped out in Israel and ruined Israel's crops by allowing their livestock to graze in Israel's fields. It got so bad that the Israelites hid in the mountains, caves, and improvised shelters. They were a people traumatized by war and living in fear. Gideon was no different. Finally, the people had lost so much that they cried out to God for help. When God called Gideon to lead the people, he was threshing grain, hiding in a winepress so the Midianites wouldn't see.

When Gideon heard the call of God, he was afraid and didn't trust that God would be with him. He felt that God had abandoned them. Gideon claimed to be too insignificant to lead because he was from the weakest clan. God had to earn Gideon's trust before Gideon would consent to lead. So Gideon asked for a sign, then another one, and finally a third sign before he finally had the courage to lead the people.

The Leader with Family Problems

My first experience with burnout followed my wife's battle with breast cancer. That year-long struggle took a toll on us all. Health problems, conflict in a marriage, a wayward child, difficult parents, or children with developmental issues can all be sources of anxiety that a leader carries everywhere they go. Some families have deep emotional or psychological problems that lead to patterns of dysfunction and codependency. If a leader doesn't have a supportive team at work, they are likely to crash. If a leader doesn't have time or space to grieve and process their pain, the very nature of these problems can make burnout inevitable.

I worked with a pastor, Anthony, whose father was an alcoholic. Anthony's mother kept making excuses for her husband. "He had such a hard childhood. . . . Things are bad for him at work. . . . He doesn't mean to be violent, it's the alcohol. . . . Don't blame your father—it's my fault." Anthony learned that his mother's codependent avoidance of the problem was the way to handle conflict.

Whenever he faced conflict as a pastor, he would fall into similar codependent patterns. Shame, anxiety, and people-pleasing behaviors were his typical response. "I don't like conflict," he told me. "It's easier for me to just go along." Anthony ended up resenting himself for being just like his mother. His critical church board became the object of his anger toward his father. He never lashed out at them, but he let his fear and anger dominate his thinking week after week. Anthony came to me when he couldn't take any more. We got him connected with a qualified therapist and began working to separate his church from his family of origin. After more than two years of work, he is able to better work through conflict and has become a true leader.

SELF-SABOTAGE

The final category of leaders likely to burn out are those prone to self-sabotage. Passionate or driven leaders are sometimes the first to fall. These leaders set high expectations and push themselves beyond their limits to achieve success. They believe it's all up to them, and their passion sustains them for a while. But when their body can no longer take the stress, passion begins to fade. Soon these leaders become frustrated by their unmet expectations. They become angry and bitter at everyone else, but they have only themselves to blame.

The Idealistic Leader

Idealistic leaders are often young and filled with a deep desire to change the world. That's what we love about them. Just being near them can be so inspiring. However, this idealistic passion can be the very thing that leads to their burnout. Idealism, by its nature, is unrealistic. Short of a miraculous work of God, it's impossible for an idealistic vision to be implemented. It's doomed to fail. And when it does, the hopes and dreams of the idealistic leader come crashing down in frustration. It's not uncommon for this leader to become cynical and hopeless as a result.

Not until I gained some perspective from recovery did I realize that my youthful idealism was a contributing factor to my burnout. I believed that because the people called me to be their pastor, they would trust me and follow my leadership. I didn't realize I needed to spend years earning their trust first. I also didn't realize that years of trust could be lost in an instant with one arrogant, selfish, or foolish action. An idealistic leader, like I was, is very likely going to burn out because of their own unrealistic expectations.

The Dreamer and Visionary

Dreamers and visionary leaders have similar problems to idealistic leaders: their hopes and dreams lead them to have unrealistic expectations. When these expectations are not met, they get frustrated and depressed. So they push even harder to meet their goals. Falling short again, they create a burnout loop of work and failure fed by their expectations.

Visionary leaders usually have a clear picture of where they want to go. However, when they lack the ability to communicate that vision to others or don't have a clear strategy to reach their goal, they drown in the details. Their followers become frustrated by their lack of clarity, which leads to uncertainty in the organization. Soon everyone is asking questions the leader can't answer. Living only in the future without planning for the present leaves a leader stranded in the sea of their vision. They often need a partner who can help them realize their vision through strategic planning and management of people and resources.

George had a wonderful vision for his church. He envisioned leading them to become a place of loving welcome to anyone who would walk through the doors. At first his congregation thought that sounded like a wonderful idea. They trained greeters, put up signage, and swapped out the hard pews for comfortable chairs that could be moved to accommodate the needs of people with disability. The congregation was taught how to welcome people without seeming needy or invading the privacy of others. They even had training on how to welcome people who were different than their white middle-class congregation.

Then different people began showing up. At first it was exciting; the church was welcoming everyone. They began to have a mix of political beliefs, races, and even LGBTQ people coming to be welcomed and loved. But as time went on, the people began to have difficulty with the varying viewpoints they were encountering. Ignorance turned to fear, and fear turned to anger. Even though George continued to maintain the theological convictions of the church and teach the gospel clearly, the congregation felt threatened.

He couldn't figure out how to help his congregation overcome their fears. Eventually, in deep fatigue and sadness he left ministry altogether.

The Disorganized Leader

Disorganized leaders probably don't come across as lazy. While they are usually quite busy, they haven't taken time to clarify their values, prioritize their work, or set boundaries for success. They try to be everything all at once because they haven't clarified their reasons for saying no to things that don't matter. By avoiding the hard work of finding clarity, they make their work harder than it needs to be. It becomes diluted by multitasking, and they drop the ball on the most important tasks because they are doing too much at once. They feel frustrated because they are doing work they should be delegating to others.

Juan was a team leader with great people skills but no administrative talent. He needed to hire an administrative assistant but could never seem to find the time to develop a job description and posting. He was missing meetings or double booking far too often. Emails went unanswered, and phone calls unreturned. Juan's team loved him as a person, but they were frustrated with his messy leadership. Soon the whole team became conflicted because Juan could not lead with clarity. Eventually, he was demoted, and now he's looking for another job.

The Divided Leader

The divided leader has broken their life into numerous categories so they can be a different person in each one. They function as one person at work and as a completely different person at church or at home. Their private life and their public life don't match. They wear so many masks it's hard to keep them all straight. Before long, one compartment starts spilling into another, and the effort to keep them all separate becomes overwhelming.

I had a friend named Eugene in my teen years who was a fellow pastor's kid. Everyone at church loved his father, Martin, and saw him as a kind, gentle man. In the home, Martin was angry and verbally abusive. Eventually, Eugene started drinking, and one day he showed up to church drunk. Eugene's father lost it in front of the whole church. He berated Eugene and blamed the church for not supporting his family. The truth came out, Martin lost his job, and both he and Eugene spent years in therapy.

PERSONALITY AND BURNOUT

This chapter is but a sampling of the types of leaders likely to burn out. Certain personality traits make burnout more likely too. If you have poor self-esteem, a strong inner critic, a propensity to avoid conflict, consistent financial problems, or unhealthy coping strategies, then you are highly likely to burn out. Introverts who are isolated and extroverts who have no deep friendships are also likely to experience burnout. In the next chapter, we will examine how a leader's inner life influences burnout. Here are some questions to help you reflect on your tendency toward burnout:

1. Where did you see yourself in the burnout profiles?
2. What is one thing you learned from this chapter about your personality and the possibility of burnout?
3. As you read this chapter, what did you sense is your deepest need right now?
4. Have you reached the point where burnout seems likely? What are the contributing factors?

3

THE INNER LIFE

On January 28, 1986, I sat in the school cafeteria as classes from several grades gathered excitedly. Released from our regular lessons, we anticipated watching the launch of the space shuttle *Challenger*. This was a rare treat, and the teachers were as giddy as the students. That day is burned into my memory forever. Just seventy-three seconds into its flight, the shuttle burst into a ball of flames. Everyone gasped and the room fell silent as we looked to our teachers for understanding. One teacher ran from the room crying. Another teacher quickly turned off the television as the others just stood there in shock, not knowing what to say. I don't remember much after that, but those few minutes are some of the clearest memories from my childhood.

We all thought *Challenger* had exploded, but that's not entirely accurate. The temperatures at launch were much colder than any previous shuttle launch—too cold. A rubber O-ring in the shuttle's right solid rocket booster had frozen, causing it to fail. This small failure allowed fire to escape out the side of the solid rocket booster (SRB). The position of the failure directed the fire like a torch toward the giant external fuel tank. The pressurized liquid hydrogen and liquid oxygen expanded as the flames superheated the tank. When the structural integrity of the tank failed, all the hydrogen and oxygen ignited at once, tearing the shuttle to pieces. The SRBs shot off in opposite directions, and the crew compartment catapulted to an altitude of 65,000 feet before falling into the Atlantic Ocean. Two minutes and forty-five seconds after the shuttle broke apart, the cabin struck the water at more than 200 miles per hour.[1]

What makes this disaster even more tragic is that it didn't have to happen. The engineers had warned command that the rubber O-rings could fail at such low temperatures, but no one heeded their warnings. Seven people lost their lives as a result. Just like the *Challenger* disaster didn't start with the O-ring failure but with an internal decision, the cause of burnout is usually unseen. It's not the external stress or the workload that ultimately causes failure. Rather, the faults in our internal life cause everything to come apart. We break down and burn out because we lose integrity.

LOSS OF INTEGRITY

When we are not in a healthy rhythm of work and renewal, we tend to divide our lives to make them more manageable. We have a work life, a home life, a private life, a public life, a thought life, a spiritual life, a prayer life, and a church life, and we think that if we can somehow keep all these things separate and in balance, we won't lose control. Dividing up our lives into pieces so we don't have to deal with the whole is called compartmentalization.[2] Sometimes compartmentalization is necessary. Soldiers on the battlefield and doctors in the emergency room are taught to compartmentalize the trauma and tragedy they experience so they can follow their training and avoid shutting down in the middle of their work. However, if they don't process the grief and trauma later, they begin to experience the effects of posttraumatic stress. So even when compartmentalization is necessary, it has potential to cause serious damage.

Unhealthy compartmentalization makes it seem like we have everything organized in nice separate boxes, but really, we've just disintegrated our lives. Author and therapist Chuck DeGroat says, "We've fractured our very selves, cutting ourselves into pieces for the roles we think we're supposed to play, each with a unique mask we think we're supposed to wear. And this inner division creates a fertile soil in which symptoms like exhaustion, burnout, perfectionism, purposelessness, anxiety, and depression can grow."[3] Maintaining this balancing act gets harder the more compartments we create. We throw ourselves into the exhausting work of trying to keep every thing in balance until eventually we run out of energy.

Leaders compartmentalize because we don't like seeing our faults, shortcomings, or sins, and we certainly don't want others to see them. We become addicted to a false image. Sin and shame like to hide in the shadows, so we dis-integrate ourselves and move the ugly parts to another box—whichever one we can avoid most easily. When we hear the word *disintegrate*, we usually think of an explosion where everything is reduced to dust and rubble. However, *disintegrate* means to "lose unity or integrity as if by breaking into parts."[4] Life should be a unified whole. That's what living with integrity means—everything in life is integrated or joined together. When we compartmentalize, we start by separating life into big chunks, but the divided life gradually disintegrates more and more. Eventually it becomes a ruin, nothing but dust and rubble. We never think that will happen to us; we're holding it together just fine.

Functional addicts are experts at living this disintegrated life. They may look like they have everything together. At first their family sees them as a good parent. They are a good worker, often excelling ahead of their peers. Their friends enjoy their company without ever realizing the dark secret: they have another, hidden life of addiction. In that life, they have a separate group of friends built around the addiction. Usually some sort of physical barrier separates this group from the other parts of the person's life. For example, these friends may be on the other side of the city, or the addict will go to meet them alone so family, coworkers, and other friends won't discover this secret life.

An alcoholic might have a favorite bar where they can meet their drinking buddies after work. He or she may tell their family they have to go on an overnight business trip when really they get out of work and spend the evening drinking, then find someplace to sleep it off. The next morning, they change into the clothes they brought for the supposed trip and go to work. Only their drinking clan will know what happened the night before. Everything appears normal if they keep their addiction hidden.

Substance addicts aren't the only ones who live disintegrated lives:

- Workaholics try to avoid the relational pain or loneliness in their life by working harder and longer.
- People in financial trouble might want to alleviate the stress, so they go on a shopping spree to get a rush of excitement. Then they hide the receipts so they won't have to deal with the reality until later.
- An intimate relationship gets rocky, so a person goes looking for another relationship to fill the gap. They replace the bad relationship with a second one, or a third one, or a fourth . . .

When we keep parts of our lives mentally and emotionally separated, we can't see how our destructive behavior hurts us in other areas. We move our sin into other boxes to avoid the pain of confronting it, but in the end, we only create more pain. Eventually, the functional addict will be discovered; no one can keep living in the tension of two lives forever. DeGroat describes how this divided life feels:

Pulled in so many different directions, we often feel we're living someone else's life, someone else's agenda, someone else's dream. We can become emotionally detached from our work, "phoning it in" and praying that the weekend comes quickly. We can sleepwalk through life, half-heartedly participating in it, depriving those we love of our full presence. Sometimes we feel as if we're living to meet the expectations of others—a spouse, a boss, a parent, a client—and we lose touch with our own longings and dreams and desires.[5]

When we feel shame and respond by compartmentalizing, we become divided, distracted, and hurried. Here are some questions to help you discern if you are living a divided life:

- Do you feel pulled in multiple directions at once?
- Are you having trouble working because you are worrying about another area of life?
- Do you find yourself rushing from one thing to another?
- Are you always running late?
- Do you feel hurried, compulsive, or neurotic?
- Are you frantically trying to improve yourself so that you can be "good enough"?
- Do you give up when you can't be perfect?
- Do you slave away for God while sacrificing your health?
- Do you have people-pleasing habits?
- When you think of your relationship with God, do you feel guilty, depressed, or insufficient?

If you answered yes to any of these, you may have a divided soul and may not be living with integrity. A compartmentalized life is not fully integrated, and that's exhausting, making it a major factor in burnout.

INTERNAL CRACKS

Leaders don't abandon their integrity for just any reason. (Again, here we're talking about structural integrity, not necessarily moral integrity.) Like in the *Challenger* disaster, the problem starts much earlier. We all suffer from internal cracks that go to our very soul that may have led us to compartmentalize our lives or divide ourselves in ways that we aren't aware of. Where do these stress fractures come from? In some cases, we have committed moral injury—choices that damage our souls by violating our own moral and ethical standards. We may be lying to ourselves. There may also be painful events or learned scripts from our past that shape us to this day. Let's explore some of the factors that shape our inner lives.

Family of Origin

One of the most influential forces that shapes your inner life is your family of origin—the family that you grew up in (whatever form that took). Your parents or other caregivers, your siblings, and how you related to one another gave you many internal pathways that you naturally follow—often without even realizing it. You might not have had a traditional family structure, but the family system in which you were raised still affected your inner life.

What were your parents like? How did they relate to each other? How did they relate to you and your siblings? Your answers may reveal some of the behaviors you learned from your family of origin. If your parents fought and yelled at each other when they had differences, you may have copied their pattern or rejected it. Either way, their behavior influenced how you live in the world.

For example, my father's temper always scared me. He didn't often lose his temper. In fact, most of my family life was filled with love and joy. But when he did get angry, even though he was never abusive, it terrified me. As a teen, I determined that I wouldn't lose my temper like my dad. So I stuffed my anger deep down where it couldn't hurt anyone—or so I thought. I reacted against my father's poor anger management with a different but equally poor strategy. Years later, my anger issues showed up as part of my burnout. I had to relearn how to manage and express anger in healthy ways. How have your relationships with your parents affected you?

Every family has learned behaviors that shape the way we live in the world. Many of those are good habits like cooking, cleaning, hygiene, and general safety. However, some may be unhealthy and even destructive. Through the influence of our parents and siblings, we can learn to be codependent, entitled, racist, or violent. Many times these learned behaviors are generational patterns that go back decades. By looking back over two, three, or even four generations of your family tree, some of these patterns will become clear.[6]

My grandfather once came home from school with a bad mark on his report card. When his mother saw it, she burst into tears, so my grandfather decided he would never have a bad report card again. Skip ahead two generations, and I learned to measure self-worth by academic success or intelligence. When we were kids, my brothers and I weren't given the answer when we had a question; we were told to "Look it up." This was long before Wikipedia or Google, so we spent hours looking things up in our deluxe set of *Encyclopedia Britannica*. While this was a good parenting strategy, and I'm thankful for the skills I learned, I also developed a negative self-image because of it. I learned intelligence was a way to earn my parents' favor, which was not the lesson they intended to teach. When people see me as smart, I feel good about myself, but if I don't have the answers, it can be crushing.

This has had its advantages. My family tends to be knowledgeable about many things; we can be serious contenders on group trivia night. We can also pick up new concepts and skills very quickly on our own.

But it has also had disadvantages. My favorite hobby is learning, but if I'm not careful, it can become a compulsion. Not everyone appreciates individuals who appear smart. I can come across as an arrogant, patronizing know-it-all, and most of the time, I'm not even aware of how I sound. Some people feel intimidated by how much I read. My family's pursuit of knowledge comes at a cost—isolation and difficulty in relationships. This was a major factor in my own burnout.

Our family of origin also shapes us through shared events. These may be positive things like vacations, religious activities, or celebrations. But how our family responded to negative events like loss, financial stress, or grief can even more deeply impact how we interact with the world. A family that suffered financial ruin may have longstanding issues around money or hoarding. A family that was betrayed by someone close may have trouble trusting others. What are the major events your family of origin faced? How have they shaped you? Are they contributing to the fractures in your inner life?

Childhood Wounds

Our inner life is also shaped by the events of our childhood, especially those times we felt wounded. In some cases, those wounds were caused by normal childhood events that for some reason affected us differently. Misinterpreting or misunderstanding an experience may have led to feelings of pain, betrayal, or abuse. Whether or not things happened as we remembered them is immaterial. What matters is *how we interpreted the events* and how that interpretation shaped our lives.

Other times we are shaped by real, painful events that we've interpreted correctly. Being bullied, having a fight with a friend or parent, or experiencing loss and grief can deeply influence us as children, causing us to put up defenses to protect ourselves from further pain. Defenses are necessary when we are young and don't have the mental capacity or life experience to process the pain. However, when they last into our adulthood they become obstacles to our growth. They prevent us from finding and living from our true self and cause soul divisions we may not even know are there.

I remember as a child being manipulated by an older kid on the playground. I had a Tony Dorsett football sticker that he wanted. He offered to trade two better stickers in return. I felt like it was a great deal for me, so I quickly offered him the sticker. He took it from my hand and walked away without giving me anything in return. When I reported the theft to the teachers, they couldn't do anything because it was my word against his. From that point, I determined I would never let people manipulate me. This childhood vow has made it hard to trust people later in life, especially when what they are offering seems too good to be true. If I even feel like I'm being manipulated, I still tend to walk away from the relationship or fight back in "righteous" anger.

What childhood vows did you make that have shaped your inner life as an adult? We've all made them, and if they remain unchallenged, they can cause cracks in our souls that will lead to a breakdown of our leadership.

Trauma and Abuse

Sometimes the cracks in our souls are caused by trauma or abuse. When our mind and soul cannot process the magnitude of what happened or what was done to us, we naturally compartmentalize the pain. Later in life, that pain begins to resurface in bits and pieces as we become better equipped to handle it. A trained professional can help make it easier to process pain. It's important to recognize that trauma or abuse may be major players in the dividing of our souls. I've worked with several leaders who acknowledged that their burnout was influenced by abusive childhood experiences coming to the surface. When they were able to work through the painful memories, they started to recover from burnout at the same time.

As I was writing the opening of this chapter and remembering the *Challenger* disaster, I realized my memories of the events didn't coincide with the dates. I remembered it happening when I was in fourth grade because it was my fourth-grade teacher who left the room in tears.

In reality, this event happened in fifth grade—a time in my life that still causes me deep pain. My fifth-grade teacher was an abusive man. He would bang kids' heads together when they were talking in class, calling it a "meeting of the minds." If he caught a student doing something wrong outside of class, he would shove their head into a locker and hold it there while shouting at them so his voice would be amplified. Why wasn't this teacher part of my memory of the *Challenger* disaster? Because whenever he could get away with it, he would abandon his class to step outside for a smoke. The abusive nature of this teacher made my whole class become defensive and abusive toward one another (as if preteens don't already have enough of that).

I may have hidden a part of me that needs to be brought out into the open to be healed, and I wonder how this is affecting my ability to lead. When I perceive someone is being verbally or physically abusive, I will stand in the gap and defend the victim. But am I really trying to defend my fifth-grade self? What if this pain from the past is causing me to misread people today? I could be projecting my fear and pain onto them—now I'm the one treating others unfairly. Can you see how unprocessed trauma may be affecting my leadership?

I realize this story may not come close to the level of abuse you've experienced, and I don't tell it by way of comparison. Each of us must process our pain in our own way. We all hide parts of ourselves to self-protect from further pain. Now, with the help of a qualified professional, we must invite these parts into the light in a safe way. As we do, we will begin to discover our true selves again.

Religion and Spirituality

Some forms of religion and spirituality push us toward the dividing of our inner world. Fundamentalist groups, no matter what religion they are part of, tend to be harsh, judgmental, and controlling. Such an environment encourages a person to develop a separate religious self. To avoid the pain of judgment, we learn to wear a religious mask, making ourselves appear holy and righteous.

Unfortunately, when we live from this false self, the wounds caused by hiding our true self will never be healed. Our sin and shame can never be brought to light because there is no safe place to do it.

If we are not welcomed with our struggles, failures, and shame, then we can't be fully human. If we are not invited into a safe place to express our pain, then our humanity isn't welcome either. This is why so many religious gatherings feel phony—everyone is hiding from everyone else under a mask of spirituality. The Christian church is supposed to be a hospital for sinners, but it ends up becoming a museum for fake saints.[7]

I should mention that not all religious experiences are bad. In fact, I believe that the Christian gospel is the only way to find one's truest self. However, the *abuse of religion* or the propagation of false teaching and unloving action creates an environment in which our souls become divided, false selves. Perhaps this is why Jesus got so mad with the false piety of the religious leaders of his day, calling them whitewashed tombs, hypocrites, or a brood of vipers. It would be easy to blame pastors and other religious leaders for this problem, and in some cases it would be warranted. However, I've found that they are just as likely to be victims of religious attacks.

There is an epidemic of hurting and abused pastors within American Christian churches, just as there's also a plague of abusive and narcissistic pastors. In my work with Pastor-in-Residence Ministries (PIR Ministries) I help pastors recover from forced exit, conflict, and burnout.[8] One pastor told me how people questioned his salvation over a small conflict after sitting under that pastor's teaching for twenty years! Another pastor was called to be the first black pastor for a campus of a multisite church, but when he challenged his narcissistic senior leader, he was let go because he "didn't fit within the culture of the church." I talk with pastors every week who have been abused by controlling elders or narcissistic senior leaders. They are deeply wounded and have a long road ahead before they can trust a church again.

Unwelcome Emotions

Sometimes we experience emotions we would rather not feel—shame, anxiety, fear, anger, sadness, depression. We tend to hide those emotions from ourselves by compartmentalizing them. We stuff them down deep, hoping they will never surface again. However, when we fail to welcome our emotions and learn from them, they continue to drain energy from us. We think we are protecting ourselves from pain, but we are creating a war within. This war between the false self that wants to hide and the true self that wants to be free will rage on until we are willing to face our emotions or until we erupt in some destructive way.

Our culture tells us that the stereotypical American male should not be emotional: he must not cry, express fear, or show any sign of "weakness." The only acceptable emotion seems to be aggressive anger. Women, on the other hand, often hide their emotions because they are likely to be seen as fragile or too sensitive, as if their emotions are too much for others to handle. It's no wonder that so many men and women today are experiencing burnout, depression, and suicidal thoughts. They don't feel free to be their true selves. It's scary to realize how many leaders are living with a false, divided self. As Chuck DeGroat says in his book *Wholeheartedness*, "To the extent that we ignore our vast inner sea with all its diversity and complexity, we inflict our dividedness on others."[9]

Relationship with Self

Ultimately the cracks in our soul are caused when we form a false self to cover up the parts of ourselves that we'd rather not see. Our facades hide painful truths by projecting more presentable images. The cracks reveal the true self attempting to break free of the lies. The true self is always working to be an integrated whole once again. Our compartmentalized or divided self cannot overcome the power of the true self. Eventually, the true self will break through as it seeks healing and wholeness.

Burnout occurs when maintaining our fractured inner life draws so much energy that we no longer have energy to maintain our outer facade. The only way forward is to bring both the true and false selves into the light to be healed. Like opening a pressure cooker, this must be done slowly, carefully, and with the help of safe people. If we move too quickly, if we aren't careful about how we do the interior work, or if we try to do it on our own, we run the risk of exploding.

DEEP WOUNDS

Some pastors cause their own exit from ministry because of moral compromise and failure. They slowly self-destruct until their secret life can no longer be hidden. They fall into addictions like pornography, alcohol abuse, sex, and other numbing behaviors. They haven't had the freedom to allow their true self to be healed. Many times this is because of a toxic religious atmosphere I described earlier. If a leader isn't free to have faults, he or she must hide their true self from the world. Eventually this becomes too much to handle, and they start looking for outlets for their pain.

I've never met a fallen pastor who wasn't deeply wounded first. This is a lesson for all leaders: we must explore our inner life and find healing, or our pain will become toxic and self-destructive as it pushes to the surface. Your inner self longs to be undivided. In part 2 we'll explore practical and actionable steps that will help you become whole and healthy.

1. We all compartmentalize or divide our lives to some degree. In what ways have you divided your life, and how has that caused a lack of integrity?
2. As you explore your internal life, consider:
   - What is your internal self-talk? Is your internal critic harsh or overactive?

- Do you feel emotionally tired, spiritually dry, or empty?
- What negative or unwanted emotions are you experiencing?
- Are you imagining fights or escapes in your daydreams?
- Are you assigning enemy status to people in your life? Why?

3. What events in your childhood led you to make a vow to live differently? What are those vows? How are your childhood vows hindering you today?

4. If you have experienced trauma or abuse, who do you need to talk with to process this pain?

5. What family scripts are you carrying with you? How does your family of origin influence you today?

4

STRESS AND BURNOUT

When it opened on July 1, 1940, the Tacoma Narrows Bridge was the third longest suspension bridge in the world.[1] Construction of the 2,800-foot bridge had started two years earlier. Everything went smoothly until they installed the road deck, and the seasoned bridge builders noticed something different about this bridge. When the wind kicked up, the bridge deck rose and fell far more than they had seen in other structures. Some movement is normal, but this bridge moved so wildly that the builders nicknamed it "Galloping Gertie."

Gertie was doomed to fail from the beginning. Everyone knew this bridge's light traffic would never generate enough revenue from tolls to pay for its construction, so before construction began, its designers made some changes to cut costs. They narrowed the road deck from four lanes to two—unusually narrow for such a long span. With a smaller, lighter deck, they could use narrow, shallow, cheap girders. These cost-saving measures spelled disaster for the bridge.

With such a lightweight foundation for the road deck, the wind bent and twisted it like ribbon. In a moderate wind, the center span rose and fell *several feet* every few seconds. At sustained winds of just thirty-five miles per hour, the road deck fell into a pattern of ever-increasing waves. The bridge builders tried reinforcing the structure with steel plates and tie-down cables. When that didn't work, they proposed making the bridge more aerodynamic by drilling holes in the girders to allow the wind to flow through. But that didn't help. Nothing worked.

On November 7, 1940, wind speeds reached forty-two miles per hour in the Tacoma Narrows, and Gertie began to gallop like never before. Leonard Coatsworth, a newspaper editor, was the last one on the bridge. As he was driving across, the rising and falling was so extreme he had to abandon his car. His dog, Tubby, refused to leave the vehicle. Leonard could hear the concrete cracking all around him as he tried to walk away. He wanted to go back for Tubby, but the bridge was moving so violently that his car was sliding back and forth across the deck. Coatsworth described the harrowing experience:

> I decided the bridge was breaking up and my only hope was to get back to shore. On hands and knees most of the time, I crawled 500 yards or more to the towers. . . . My breath was coming in gasps; my knees were raw and bleeding, my hands bruised and swollen from gripping the concrete curb. . . . Towards the last, I risked rising to my feet and running a few yards at a time. . . . Safely back at the toll plaza, I saw the bridge in its final collapse and saw my car plunge into the Narrows.[2]

Just like the Tacoma Narrows Bridge, a leader will collapse in burnout when their internal structure cannot sustain the external pressures of their work and life. Most burnout is caused by two interior faults: anxiety and shame. But before we can investigate them in detail, we need to understand the external stresses that expose them in the life of a leader.

STRESS

Stress is a term engineers use to describe external physical force or pressure exerted on an object. Stress can be good or bad. When building large structures like bridges, engineers talk about six types of stress: compression, tension, shear, bending, torsion, and fatigue. When designing a suspension bridge or cable stay bridge, engineers rely on tension to hold everything in place. The downward force of gravity on the roadbed is transferred into the towers by the tension in the cables. These towers, in turn, are under compression to transfer the weight of the road and the cables into the bedrock below the waterline. This is an example of good stress because it provides stability to the bridge and a safe way across the divide.

In the same way, there are good stresses in our lives. A deadline can provide motivation to do work in a timely manner. Friendly competition can push us to grow. Weight-bearing exercise will help us get stronger. Each of these stresses is good within limits. However, when we exceed those limits, we suffer physical, emotional, or spiritual injury. The Yerkes-Dodson Law states that as stress increases so does performance, but only up to a point. Once we've reached peak performance, increased stress will produce diminishing results until we end up in a chronic condition like burnout. Notice the bell curve of performance and stress in the diagram below.[3]

FIGURE 1   YERKES DODSON LAW

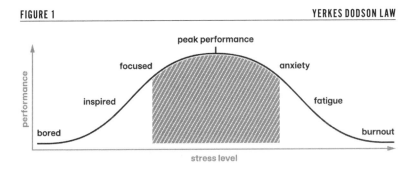

I loved playing basketball in my teen years. My best friend, Jason, and I were evenly matched, and our friendly competition pushed each of us to get better. One spring we decided to recruit a couple of friends and enter a three-on-three tournament (one player was on the bench as a substitute). It was a double elimination tournament, so when we lost our first game, we found ourselves in the losers' bracket. We went on to win every subsequent game and earned a place in the finals, where we faced the team we had lost to initially. We were out for revenge. It was the most intense game of basketball I've ever played. We gave it our all and pushed ourselves well beyond responsible physical limits.

In the end, we lost more than just the final game. I spent the next three months in physical therapy for a severely strained back. I had to lie on my back during my high school classes when the pain got too intense—which didn't help my popularity with students or teachers. Jason was worse off than me. As a nose tackle in football, he had previously fractured a vertebra in his neck, and even though his neck had healed, our game aggravated that injury. Soon after the tournament, he began to suffer headaches, memory issues, and other symptoms that lasted for years. We had stressed our bodies beyond the breaking point.

Stress becomes a problem when it is too great or lasts too long. Like the materials tested by engineers, we reach our breaking point. Knowing this limit is helpful, but continually pushing that limit is dangerous. Imagine an architect designing a building that pushes every material to just short of its breaking point. Would you want to live in that building? A small breeze or added weight (like furniture or people) could cause the building to come crashing down. In the same way, no one likes being around a leader who is continually pushing themselves and their team to the extreme. It can be exciting until somebody breaks, and then everyone suffers.

Burnout becomes more likely the longer we live near our breaking point. Do you know your limits? Where are your physical, mental, emotional, and spiritual breaking points? Below are six engineering terms for stress that serve as metaphors for ministry or leadership stress. As you read each one, try to remember times when you were under this type of stress. Did any of them cause you to reach your breaking point?

1. **COMPRESSION:** Force pressing down or in, which causes us to feel squeezed or trapped by work or ministry. It can come from having too many bosses, unrealistic expectations, or too much pressure to perform. We feel smaller, and eventually, we are crushed or buckle under the pressure. People pleasers often suffer from this kind of stress.

2. **TENSION:** The stress of being pulled in two or more directions so that it feels like there is not enough of us to go around. We may feel like we need more hours, more energy, or more compassion than we have available. Tension will make us feel stretched out and unable to bounce back. This type of stress can come from not saying no. It's a sign that we lack healthy margin in our lives.

3. **SHEAR:** A single, high-stress event that leaves one broken and unable to move on. Depending on the nature of this event, posttraumatic stress may become a reality. The trauma of shearing stress can linger for years if we don't get professional help.

4. **BENDING:** Stress that pushes us beyond our normal tolerance levels and leaves us feeling permanently weakened. We will likely require additional support to recover from this stress. Chronic overworking, toxic work cultures, and people pleasing are among the many sources of bending stress.

5. **TORSION:** Stress that twists us around and around. Deep misunderstanding or a sudden awareness of a leadership blind spot causes us to become disoriented and to feel like we need a new understanding of the situation (or the world) to move forward.

6. **FATIGUE:** Prolonged stress that slowly wears us down until we break, usually in a catastrophic way. This *allostatic load*, or continual weight, becomes too much for too long. Even a light weight can become too heavy over time. This type of stress comes from a lack of healthy boundaries and restorative rest.

Which of these stresses are you experiencing right now? Burnout happens when one or more of them exceed our capacity. The problem isn't in our weakness but in our trying to have more strength than God has supplied. When we push beyond the threshold God has set, we burn out.

HOW STRESS EXPOSES OUR FAULTS

Many people assume that burnout is caused by working too hard. More than one pastor I've coached has said something like, "I'm not sure how much longer I can last. I haven't had a Sunday off in five years." At first glance, you might think this burnout was caused by overworking and a lack of rest. However, if we are brave enough to dig down to the root cause of our burnout, it's rarely overwork. Steve Cuss, author of *Managing Leadership Anxiety*, says, "Burnout has less to do with workload and more to do with internal and external leadership anxiety."[4]

When we begin to do the hard work of getting to the cause of our burnout, it can be a bit like peeling an onion. At first we think overwork is the cause, but if we dig deeper with the help of a friend, coach, or counselor, we will begin to see something behind our overwork. Maybe it's driven by people pleasing or by wanting to avoid trouble at home. Whatever the root cause, there is always a deeper issue behind overwork.

As I explored the cause of my own burnout, I found layers of people pleasing, unrealistic expectations, a need for praise that went back to my childhood, chronic anxiety, and shame. A lot of shame. I didn't know these were factors until I peeled back the layers.

Over the next few pages, we will look at twelve case studies on the causes of burnout. (Note that this is not an exhaustive list. There are far more sources for burnout than can be explored in one book.) These studies highlight the two most common causes of burnout: anxiety and shame.[5] Under these two categories, I've listed six ways each can lead to burnout. You may be tempted to skim through these quickly, but a slower, more reflective approach will yield greater wisdom. As we slowly walk through each case, examine your internal world. Take note of which cases resonate the most with you; these may be layers in your own burnout.

Anxiety

Chronic anxiety is the common thread in our first six cases. Steve Cuss says that "anxiety is generated when we think we need something in a particular moment that we don't actually need."[6] In most cases, anxiety tells us the lie that we are missing something. When we embrace that lie, it leads to desperation or despair. In each of the following cases, ask yourself these four questions: What is the lie that the leader has embraced? What does this person think they need? What truth or affirmation would set this person free? How do I see myself in this case?

Anxiety Case 1: Assumptions

"I thought ministry would be easier," said Jared. "Seminary didn't prepare me for all these angry people. I can't believe the way people in my church treat one another. I assumed working with Christians would be easier than my other jobs. These people are worse! What should I do?"

Assumptions can be deadly to a leader. When we imagine how things are going to go based on our assumptions, we will almost always be disappointed. We usually aren't even aware of our assumptions until something goes wrong. We feel devastated when life and leadership don't function the way we imagined they would. We thought we had the world figured out, but now we realize we don't have a clue. Every leader experiences this from time to time, but a major episode of cognitive dissonance based on faulty assumptions can create intense anxiety. If we can't live in the present moment and navigate our way to the truth, living with instability will make the anxiety chronic and pervasive—fertile ground for burnout.

Anxiety Case 2: Expectations

"You want the impossible!" Sharon screamed. Judy didn't think she was asking too much. She believed her daughter was capable of getting top grades. If only she would apply herself a little more, Sharon could be valedictorian in a few years. Judy couldn't understand why this was such a big deal to Sharon, and it was keeping her up at night.

Unrealistic expectations for yourself or others is an on-ramp to chronic anxiety. When we hold ourselves to superhuman ideals, the pressure to perform is always with us. This can lead to feelings of inadequacy, internal criticism, and anger. When we hold others to high expectations that they themselves do not hold, we become controlling and manipulative. Soon people will begin to resent us or feel like they are walking on eggshells around us. The anxiety fog of unrealistic expectations will hang in the air everywhere we go.

Anxiety Case 3: Dreams and Passions

"But I love my job!" Joe objected when Randy, his therapist, suggested he take some time off. "It's all I've ever wanted to do. I can't leave now. Besides, vacation is so boring." Randy replied, "Joe, what does it tell you that you can't take two weeks to do whatever you want other than work?"

Joe's overattachment to his work comes from the fact that he really does love it. Sometimes our dreams and passions can become all-consuming. When we lack healthy boundaries in our work, we lose the activities that help us release stress. Just because you love your job doesn't mean it will be stress free. In fact, loving your work may make the stress feel closer and more personal. The more passionate we are about our work, the more likely we are to push our limits and burn the candle at both ends. We all need healthy separation between our work and our personal identity. When it is hard to distance yourself from the source of anxiety, burnout has already begun.

Anxiety Case 4: Financial Pressures

"Just put it on the credit card. We'll pay it off when we can." Shawna's business wasn't growing like she had expected. Two years had passed since she quit her job to start a food truck. While the finances for the business were improving, she was still in the red every month. To make the business viable, she borrowed from her family's savings. Now, as she looks ahead, it will be at least one or two more years before this business starts turning a profit. In the meantime, her debts keep growing.

The pressures of debt and financial juggling can become over-whelming. The bills never stop coming; they are like monthly anxiety generators. One or two bad months can be devastating if you are living paycheck to paycheck. Chronic anxiety in this case makes it feel like you will never get ahead. This hopelessness is one indicator of burnout.

Anxiety Case 5: Conflict

"Maybe it will just go away." This was David's standard response to conflict—avoid it at all costs. "If it doesn't go away on its own, I'll talk to Jim." David was upset over Jim's recent habit of waiting until the last minute to assign David a task. Now the job was urgent and would require David to stay late to get it done in time. When David confronted Jim, things got heated. Jim said, "Alright, I'll get it to you earlier. Stop being so sensitive!" This resolved the problem but introduced further tension into their relationship. What David didn't realize was that he was carrying that conflict everywhere he went. Jim may have let it go, but David couldn't, and it was eating him up.

Conflict always creates anxiety. Unresolved conflict drains leaders. Leaders who avoid conflict usually don't know how to deal with it in healthy ways. They haven't learned how to work through conflict to get positive results. What should be an opportunity to grow together becomes a source of division that infects the relationship at all levels. These conflicts usually occur because of competing vision, unstated values, compromised priorities, assumed motives, or violated boundaries. Sometimes people are overly aggressive to push conflict and drive others away while others may be passive-aggressive, letting their anger simmer on the surface. Unresolved conflict creates a growing cancer of chronic anxiety: it can't be ignored for long. Relational conflict burns off our internal resources and leaves us feeling hollow and tired.

Anxiety Case 6: Toxic Cultures

"It's never enough!" Susie was a vice president in a large company known for its toxic culture. The CEO, Miguel, was a highly driven and critical leader. No matter how good Susie's team performed, Miguel was never satisfied. He could always find something wrong or make them feel like they should have done better. If they met their goals, he just assumed the goals were too low to begin with. It seemed like he wasn't happy until someone else felt bad. This made everyone in the company reserved and unwilling to take risks. The other VPs tried to protect their department by throwing one another under the bus. Susie could feel the anxiety rise in her body every day on her drive to the office.

Susie wasn't the cause of her anxiety; she was the victim of a toxic leader and a toxic work environment. The only thing Susie did wrong was staying where she wasn't appreciated. Working in this type of environment can be traumatic. It's like dying from thousands of paper cuts—every criticism takes a little life away. A critical workplace creates a constant fear response until soon everyone is in a state of hypervigilance. An anxious group creates a vortex of anxiety that can burn out of control.

Shame

Anxiety and shame are usually inseparable; they feed off each other. When we feel anxious, our personal identity and unique way of showing up in the world are threatened. We can be tempted to withdraw, put on a mask, or become aggressive, which are all ways we lose our confident, brave, healthy self. If you look back over the previous six case studies, you can probably see how each person's anxiety contributed to shame or a loss of self. Curt Thompson, author of *The Soul of Shame*, says:

> Researchers have described shame as a feeling that is deeply associated with a person's sense of self, apart from any interactions with others; guilt, on the other hand, emerges as a result of something I have done that negatively affects someone else. Guilt is something I feel because I have done something bad. Shame is something I feel because I am bad.[7]

So shame is a rejection of self that leads to isolation from others for fear that they will see how bad we are. We imagine that others will hate, judge, or reject us (usually despite evidence to the contrary). Try to recognize how shame and getting wrapped up in the emotions and judgments of others may be contributing to your burnout. It may be helpful to ask the following questions as you read each of the next six cases: In what way has this person lost their individuality? How are the opinions, judgments, or emotions of others invading the person's heart or mind? What boundaries or disciplines would help this person find freedom? How do I see myself in this case?

Shame Case 1: Limits and Boundaries

"Why did I agree to do this?" Sara asked herself. She just couldn't say no and once again was in over her head. She can't possibly do everything people expect of her. She often wonders, "When will I get some time to do what I want to do?" Sara has been this way all her life. She believes it's because her mother was so demanding and manipulative that she feels guilty if she doesn't say yes.

Sara doesn't know where she ends and someone else begins. She is trying to manage other people's emotions by agreeing to whatever they ask. At the same time, Sara isn't aware of her own needs and desires. Saying yes keeps her busy, which means she doesn't have to deal with her own pain. Leaders like Sara usually burn out multiple times. For example, their burnout may show up as recurring sickness whenever they try to slow down. They begin to resent everyone around them for being so demanding. However, it's their own inability to establish healthy boundaries that hurts them. These leaders are their own worst enemy.

Shame Case 2: Trauma and Grief

Yasmeen kept to herself most of the time. She had been abused by her father as a child and didn't want to be in a place where she felt vulnerable. So she did everything she could to control her environment and the people in it. Then her mother, her protector, died, and Yasmeen felt like she would never be safe again. Rather than grieving her loss, Yasmeen put on a tough exterior and pretended everything was fine. Everyone wondered why she seemed angry all the time.

Failing to grieve our losses and process our trauma in healthy ways creates an ever-present stress that becomes the background noise of our lives. We try to control everyone and everything because we don't feel safe. This makes other people resent us, and we quickly become tired. We may feel like the people we love are abandoning us again, but in reality, we are pushing them away by making it impossible for them to get close. Our actions and our desires are in direct contradiction. Not everyone who has been abused or trauma-tized responds this way, but those who do create a friction that sparks their own burnout.

Shame Case 3: Sexuality and Body Issues

Jon is a kind and gentle man, not aggressive or angry like the cultural stereotypes tell him he should be. In his early years, the other boys would ask, "What's wrong with you? Are you gay or something?" This led Jon to fake aggressiveness in sports and in his relationships, which made him feel like a fraud. To deal with this emotion, Jon would eat foods that made him feel good . . . and gain weight. As an adult, he prefers the company of women because they appreciate his gentle ways, but his weight makes him feel unattrac-tive. He often wonders if God made a mistake in making him.

Cultural stereotypes around gender, sexuality, and body can cre-ate intense pressure to conform to a group. When people experience this kind of stress, they often internalize shame and feel excluded from community. Rather than working through the issues, they may be tempted to join any group that makes them feel "normal"—especially if that group is countercultural. Unfortunately, the stress will always be with them until they learn to value their body, treat themselves with compassion, and pursue healthy habits.

Shame Case 4: Isolation

"I'm so lonely. No one understands what it's like to be in my position." Tuan was a good leader. Everyone thought he was at the top of his game. He had a dynamic personality and a large following. However, to maintain his influence, Tuan couldn't let anyone see his doubts or struggles. Every day Tuan put on a smile. All the while he was dying inside. He had no friends—no one who knew and loved the real Tuan. He was on a deserted island of his own making.

Isolation is what happens when we don't have friends or mentors who can ask us hard questions. We all need people who love us for who we are and who are willing to challenge us because they love us. We trust these people to have our best interests in mind. These people don't want anything from us but friendship. They help us become the best versions of ourselves, and we can be open and honest with them. When we resist this type of vulnerability, isolation becomes inevitable. Leadership, by its very nature, can be lonely. When the leader feels they can't be real or human, this loneliness morphs into deep isolation. Where can this leader turn when life becomes too much? Who will help them douse the flames of burnout?

Shame Case 5: Spiritual Dryness and Doubt

"I think I'm losing my faith," said Isaiah as we talked over coffee. "I just don't believe in the same way I used to." Isaiah's crisis of faith stemmed from a time of spiritual dryness—what some Christians refer to as a dark night of the soul. It's a period where one's spiritual practices are no longer life-giving and refreshing. Isaiah struggled to hold on to the last shreds of faith, and he doubted they would sustain him. He didn't have much strength left.

Spiritual doubt creates anxiety because we feel like we've lost ourself. The faith that used to define us no longer seems sufficient. While this may be a necessary step in our spiritual growth, it often feels like death. The grief associated with this loss can become overwhelming. As we get lost in the search for stability, we have trouble focusing at work or at home. Only time will tell if our faith is strong enough to sustain us through this period. In this case, burnout often causes people to walk away from their faith for a time (and sometimes for a lifetime).

Shame Case 6: Negative Self-Talk

The embarrassment was overwhelming. "How could I be so stupid?" Emma asked. "If the people I lead found out about this, they would call me a fraud." Emma was the leader of a nonprofit dedicated to feeding the poor and homeless in her community. She was running late for work when a panhandler started to "wash" her windshield. She yelled at the man and cursed him before driving away. As the day went on, Emma continued to berate herself and relive the event in her mind. Rather than focusing on what she could do differently next time, she ruminated on her failure and how she could keep it hidden from others.

Emma's experience, which is common to leaders, is called *imposter syndrome*. It's the feeling that your leadership is a fraud and that you have no business being in this position. Shame in the form of negative self-talk drives the leader deeper and deeper into anxiety, fear, and depression. Like a self-fulfilling prophecy, the fear of being seen as a fraud causes the leader to put up a false front and isolate from others. Like most forms of shame, imposter syndrome is a lie. However, when we begin to believe this lie, we lose the confidence we need to lead well.

Shame is the fuel that feeds the inferno of burnout. It's often the source of our anxiety and loss of self. Usually rooted in childhood or in memories that have been repressed for years, shame becomes the driving force behind people-pleasing, a lack of healthy boundaries, isolation, and so many of the things that contribute to burnout. Curt Thompson says, "We are only as sick as the secrets we keep. And shame is committed to keeping us sick."[8] The secrets we keep from ourselves and others feed the shame cycle. This downward cycle makes us feel drained, lost, and afraid.

STRESS, ANXIETY, AND SHAME

In the next chapter we will learn how our energy and rhythms of work and rest influence burnout. For now, consider the three factors that can contribute to burnout: stress, anxiety, and shame. Knowing about these concepts is a good start, but if you want to recover from burnout, you will need a deeper level of understanding. Some people are able to uncover this on their own, but most need the help of a trusted friend, spiritual director, mentor, or therapist. Don't be afraid to ask for help. Here are a few questions to help to see what stresses may be causing fractures in your leadership that could lead to burnout.

1. How is stress operating in your life right now? Is it healthy stress that drives you to grow, or is it harmful stress? Name the harmful stress you are experiencing.
2. In which of the twelve case studies of burnout causes did you see yourself?
3. Make a list of the contributing factors in your own burnout that this chapter has helped you discover.
4. What secrets are you keeping? Take some time for quiet meditation to explore if you are keeping secrets from yourself. Who can you talk with to help you uncover these secrets?
5. Tell the story of your burnout (write it out or tell it to a trusted friend). What were you surprised to hear yourself say?

5

ENERGY AND RHYTHMS

Japan, the most seismically active country on earth, averages 160 noticeable earthquakes per year, so the Japanese people are used to feeling the ground shake. But at 2:46 p.m. on March 11, 2011, they experienced the strongest recorded earthquake in the nation's history.[1] A quake measuring 9.1 on the Richter scale shook the Tōhoku region for almost six minutes as wave after wave of energy pulsated through the earth. When quiet finally descended, the people began digging out of the debris. Little did they know, this calm would last only nine minutes.

Forty-five miles offshore and fifteen miles beneath the surface, the quake's epicenter released a tremendous amount of energy into the ocean. This triggered Japan's tsunami warning system, which registered a series of ten-foot waves rushing toward the coast at nearly five hundred miles per hour. Sirens wailed throughout the region and people began running for high ground. As the waves approached shore, the rising seabed dramatically slowed the leading wave. Like a multicar pileup on the highway, the trailing waves pushed into the decelerating lead wave and merged with it, causing the water to rise to an unfathomable height. The gargantuan wave grew, pulling water away from the shore as waves do. It might have looked like the tide was going out, but the water retreated farther and faster than any low tide.

Just thirty minutes after the earthquake hit, a thirty-three-foot wall of water crashed over the eighteen-foot seawall. In flat areas the water pushed inland as far as six miles. In areas where the ground rose steeply from the shoreline, the tsunami crested up to 128 feet above sea level! Its enormous mass pushed buildings off their foundations, leveling entire cities and towns. As the water retreated into the sea, it pulled more than five million tons of debris into the ocean. Japan suffered a $220 billion loss from this natural disaster, and 98 percent of that is attributed to the tsunami.

A tsunami behaves much like other waves but with one critical exception: wind-generated waves only travel on the water's surface, while a tsunami goes all the way to the ocean floor. Like other waves, a tsunami starts as a series of smaller waves with peaks and troughs. All waves have a rhythm. A wave's leading edge is a low point as water particles are pulled into the coming peak. The energy pushing the wave, whether in the form of the wind or an earthquake, causes the water to rise and creates another trough behind the peak. Scientists measure waves based on this series of peaks and troughs. The higher and wider the wave peaks, the lower and wider the troughs and the more energy transmitted.

If you are at the beach on a calm day, you will see small rolling waves spaced far apart and ideal for swimming and playing. If a storm approaches, the waves will grow higher and bunch closer together. Soon the rhythm of the waves becomes so rapid and their power so intense that riptides form, pulling water from the shore to feed the energy of the storm-driven waves. Trying to swim in this kind of rhythm is exhausting and can be life-threatening.

Just as ignoring the intensity of physical waves can be dangerous to swimmers, ignoring life's natural rhythms of energy can be dangerous to leaders. For many leaders, all their energy flows in one direction all the time. Like a tsunami, their energy keeps flowing until nothing is left, and they only rest once their energy is depleted. Tsunami leaders are much more likely to burn out. Their hard-charging, high-energy leadership is great for a while. People love to follow this type of leader, but their intensity can only carry them so far. They fill up their calendar and cram as much as they can into every minute. They have little margin because they believe rest is a waste of time. One such leader even told me, "I can sleep when I'm dead!" This constant push forward may feel productive, but there is a better way of leading.

The alternating peaks and troughs of waves provide a metaphor for this better way; good leadership has rhythms of work and rest. Energy out *and* energy in. Healthy leaders understand that time management is actually energy management and that there are different types of energy that need to be managed. In this chapter, we will explore how ignoring our God-given limits and the natural rhythms of life can cause a leader to burn out.

BURNOUT AND ENERGY MANAGEMENT

How do you manage your time? Leaders who burn out usually operate as tsunami leaders. They lay out their calendar of available time, fill it up with what needs to get done, and never consider how much physical, emotional, and spiritual energy they have available at any given moment. They rarely look at how certain parts of their vocation take more energy and leave them drained. After these draining tasks, they enter important meetings or responsibilities with less energy than the job requires.

When we are young, we can work harder for longer periods of time. However, as we get into our thirties and forties, that type of work takes a heavier toll on our bodies. When I was in college, I could work through the night writing a paper for class and get through the next day with only a short nap. Now that I'm in my mid-forties, I wouldn't even attempt that. It would leave me depressed for days because my body can't recover as quickly as it used to. My experience of burnout taught me that I was no longer a young man. I needed to carefully observe myself and my life to notice how my energy levels changed through the days and seasons.

Healthy leaders look at time management not as a calendar to fill but as an energy budget to spend. They consider the physical, emotional, and spiritual drain of each task. They prioritize tasks and meetings that are most important so they can bring their best energy to them. When they have a job that is particularly draining, they purposefully schedule time for recovery—intentional margin in their calendars that prevents the drain of that task from infecting other parts of their job. Healthy leaders recognize they have only so much energy and therefore need to find an alternating rhythm of work and rest to bring their best self to their most important work.

Noticing Energy Rhythms

We can't live at a constant rate of output. Like the rest of creation, we need periods of rest and restoration. Everywhere we look in nature, we observe rhythms around us and within us. Waves, wind, heartbeats, and breathing all function in rhythms, with natural pauses for rest and energy renewal. However, as philosopher and cultural theorist Byung-Chul Han observes, "Today we live in a world that is very poor in interruption; 'betweens' and 'between-times' are lacking."[2] We continue our hard-charging ways, ignoring the necessary periods of rest between the heartbeats.

Like the ocean waves, our energy levels have peaks and troughs that cycle throughout our days and seasons. Each of us experience these highs and lows. For example, you've probably felt your energy crash around midafternoon. You know you'll get a second wind later in the day, so you tell yourself, "I just need to push through this."

Think about your energy rhythms. At what point in your day do you feel most energized? When is your energy at its lowest? My low points are often the early morning and midafternoon. I struggle to get going in the morning as my body and mind take about an hour to fully wake up. Sometimes I can force this with a rush of adrenaline from the stress of an early appointment, but I know I will feel exhausted by lunchtime. Likewise, my energy plummets around midafternoon from the after-lunch push to get things done. These are *my* energy cycles. Yours may look different, but we all have them.

Peaks and Troughs

Let's continue with our wave metaphor. Have you ever watched the waves at the ocean or on the Great Lakes? After a peak hits the shore, it's followed by a trough, a space where there is less water flowing. In fact, the peaks and troughs are usually equal. The troughs will be as deep as the peaks are high and just as wide. Even when the wind is pushing the waves toward shore, the troughs are there. While the peaks are taller, hit the shore closer together, and push farther up the beach, the troughs become deeper and narrower, and the undercurrent becomes stronger. If those peaks and troughs weren't in balance, the water would flood the land.

In a hurricane or tsunami, the volume of water flowing onto land is greater than the undercurrent can handle. But even such a huge wave or storm surge pushing into shore for such an extended period has an equally massive trough before and after it. First the water retreats from the land. Then the wave or surge rolls in, destroying everything in its path. Finally, the water retreats into the ocean where the rhythms of the waves return to normal.

Sometimes leadership requires tsunamis of energy for a period. Leaders who burn out after these periods haven't learned that before and after every big surge, they need down times when their body, mind, and soul can prepare or recover.

Think of a wave as a picture of our energy output. In complete calm, the water is flat—no peaks or troughs. This is our baseline. The peaks that form above the line represent periods of output. They may be physical output like running or lifting weights. They may be emotional output like grief or intense joy. Times of high stress and even spiritually intense experiences are both forms of energy output.

FIGURE 2   WAVE RHYTHM

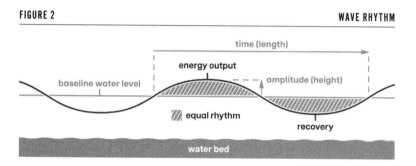

Whenever we need to expend energy, our body, mind, and soul need an equal amount of time to recover. The troughs below the baseline represent these recovery periods. Here's the principle that most burned-out leaders haven't learned: *the amount of your output equals the amount of recovery you need.* We must consider both the time (length of the wave) and the amplitude (height of the wave) in our energy output. If we consider the area of each wave and trough as amplitude multiplied by time, the area below the baseline will need to equal the area above the baseline for energy recovery. So if the recovery period is less in amplitude, it will have to last a longer time. The recovery trough will appear flatter but contain the same amount of area under the baseline. Perhaps a few examples will help illustrate this.

Consider a marathon runner. They don't run a marathon every day. Leading up to the day of the race, they condition their body through periods of training and recovery as they work up to the full 26.2 miles. After running the marathon, they need days to recover. As their muscles heal from the damage, runners replenish their energy stores by eating healthy foods, getting quality sleep, and avoiding strenuous activity. Their very high output is followed by low output as they rest and recover. The amplitude of their output is one intense day of physical and mental endurance, but their recovery time lasts several days as their body needs time to repair itself.

FIGURE 3   MARATHONER AND SPRINTER RHYTHM

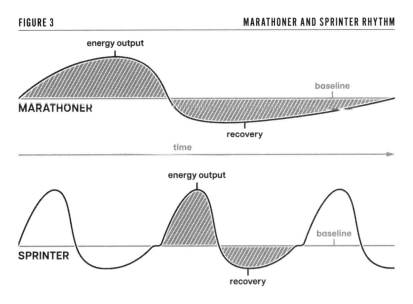

A sprinter, on the other hand, will put out a vast amount of energy over a very short time and distance. They run fast but not for long. Their recovery time is also quicker, and they can run several events in one day. A marathon runner goes slower to go farther. A sprinter could never sprint a whole marathon, yet many leaders treat their work like a daily and weekly sprint. Then they wonder why they collapse into burnout.

In my work as a pastor, I was honored to officiate funerals. Each funeral required several hours of extra work and emotional output. I learned early on that I couldn't just add on the emotional weight and stress of caring for a grieving family to my already heavy workload.

So I took an extra day off the week following the funeral. That would be my time to grieve and recover. However, the stress of these events often lasted several weeks because my work schedule was overloaded, and I didn't have enough margin to absorb that extra time and energy. It usually took me an extra week to catch up and two more weeks to recover my energy levels. During that time, I was living in the trough and felt mildly depressed, but I knew this was just my body and soul recovering.

Energy Deficit

Leaders burn out when they are deficit spending on their energy budget. They don't allow their recovery time to match their energy output. This results in less energy available for the next stressful event because they are still paying interest on the first one. Each expenditure perpetuates the cycle until, because of insufficient recovery, they soon run out of energy. They are living with the weight of constant anxiety and shame. Simply getting out of bed in the morning feels like a monumental task. They become depressed and burned out as their body tells them it needs time to recover.

If you ignore your body's need for rest, it may push you into forced recovery through illness, injury, depression, or burnout. I'm convinced one of the key reasons for the ever-increasing rates of stress-related illness and depression among leaders is because we haven't learned the principle of recovery. We aren't giving ourselves enough time to recover and feel secure or at ease after stressful events. So the stress cycle never ends, and we carry today's stress into tomorrow, next week, and next year.

Intentional rhythms of rest and recovery alone won't stop burnout from happening, but failure to rest and recover will make burnout inevitable. Chronic anxiety and shame are like a tsunami. As the water finally recedes from the shore, we have nothing left to give. They drain our internal resources. Chronic anxiety and shame leave destruction in their wake.

WHAT ARE YOUR RHYTHMS?

Are you aware of the life rhythms you must adopt to be your best, most energized self? Take a moment and notice your breathing. Inhale deeply through your nose. Notice the cool air filling your lungs. Do you feel more energy as you breathe in? Open your mouth and exhale. Notice the warm, moist air passing out of your body. As you exhale, do you notice how your body feels slightly depleted and ready for the next breath? Try waiting several seconds before you inhale. Notice how this feeling becomes more intense with each second that passes.

Now put two fingers on your wrist or your neck to check your pulse. Can you feel it? Our bodies rely on a healthy sinus rhythm of breathing, pumping blood, and rest to survive. These natural rhythms happen many times every minute. What would it be like if your heart didn't rest between beats? Twice I've had a panic attack. My heart was racing so fast I thought I was having a heart attack. It felt like I was going to die from too many heartbeats. When my normal rhythm returned, I was both relieved and exhausted. Normal rhythms are good!

We also have daily rhythms. Every day we need food, water, sleep, and hygiene. We may be able to skip these for a day or two, but eventually we have to return to healthy rhythms or we become ill. What we eat and the quality of our sleep have a profound impact on our body's ability to function. Leaders who eat unhealthy food or who don't get at least seven hours of sleep each night are much more likely to burn out, feel depressed, or get sick—all signs that their recovery rhythms are out of balance. Cutting corners on healthy eating or sleep makes us less productive over time. Such so-called time savers are really energy drains.

Just as the body has natural and daily rhythms, we also have rhythms for our mind, emotions, relationships, and spiritual life. These rhythms affect the energy we bring to each moment. In later chapters, I will give you tools to help you establish healthy rhythms. For now, it's important to notice what your current rhythms look like. Here are some questions to help you chart where you may be losing energy.

- Are you eating good, healthy meals at regular intervals throughout the day?
- How did what you ate today make you feel in the hours after each meal or snack?
- Are you getting seven to eight hours of quality, deep sleep each night?
- When during the day do you feel most energized? Why do you feel energy at these points?
- When during the day do you feel least energized? Again, why is this happening?
- What type of work energizes or excites you?
- What parts of your job or leadership are draining to you?
- What are you doing to bring your best energy to your most important work?
- Are there times of the day, week, or year when you experience more intense emotions? What are those emotions, when do they occur, and why do you think they show up at this time?
- How do your spiritual rhythms affect your emotions and energy levels throughout the week?
- When do you feel most hurried? Why?
- How do you feel when you relax? Why?
- What are your habits of physical exercise and hygiene? How do these impact your energy levels?

These are just a few of the ways you can explore how you may be moving toward burnout. Are you a tsunami leader, always pushing and never resting? Or are you a healthy leader, with intentional rhythms of work and recovery? Are you running at a constant sprint, or are you slowing down so you can run farther? When you think about your life, do you feel energized or exhausted? Do you feel joy or dread?

THE RHYTHMS OF JESUS

In Matthew 11:28–30, Jesus says, "Come to me, all you who are weary and burdened, and I will give you rest. Take my yoke upon you and learn from me, for I am gentle and humble in heart, and you will find rest for your souls. For my yoke is easy and my burden is light." Many people implicitly interpret this text to say that we should come to Jesus after we've exhausted ourselves through hard work. Others believe that it means we need to trust Jesus to make our heavy work—our stressful schedules and overburdened jobs—a little easier to carry. I believe *Jesus is giving us a completely different way of understanding work.*[3]

A yoke is a large piece of wood attached to a working animal so it can pull a cart or a plow. Some yokes enable two animals to work side by side. In Jesus's time, a farmer would use one or two oxen to plow the fields. A young ox singly yoked to a plow would pull against the plow with all his might. He would go fast at first but quickly lose steam. If the farmer wasn't careful, the young ox would work himself to death.

To prevent this from happening, the farmer would use a double yoke and pair the young ox with an older, more mature ox that had learned to go at the slow and steady pace of the farmer. By going slow, both ox and farmer would have enough energy to finish plowing the field. By yoking the young, inexperienced ox with the mature ox, the farmer trains him to slow down so he can learn to plow at the farmer's pace, not his own.

Jesus is telling us to become yoked to him and to let him teach us his slow ways—the ways that make the burden lighter and easier. In the larger context of the passage, Jesus highlights his meekness and gentle spirit. He teaches us to go at the pace of the farmer (God the Father). We can learn much from Jesus if we are willing to walk with him.

When I was in the depths of my burnout, I learned the lesson of being yoked to Jesus. I had been living as a young, foolish ox, charging ahead with no awareness of my limits and my need for rest and recovery. Alan Fadling says, "Hard work and effort are good, God-given capacities, but when these become separated from a living communion with God, they can become destructive rather than constructive."[4] My burnout became the gift that taught me to slow down to go far. I learned to honor my limits and found a rhythm of work and rest that made me more productive and enabled me to bring more of my true self to my work. My work became easier, more joyful, and exciting once again.

As we read the Gospels, it's easy to see Jesus busily working as he preaches to crowds, heals people, and even skips meals to focus on the needs of others. However, if we focus only on the busy work of Jesus, we will miss the source of his energy for this work. Jesus practiced regular rhythms of rest and prayer before and after these high-output situations.

Luke 5:16 describes Jesus's custom of rest and prayer: "But Jesus often withdrew to lonely places and prayed." Notice that Jesus didn't just rest; he withdrew and prayed. Jesus found places that recharged his soul like a mountain top (Mark 6:46) or a garden (John 18:1). Sometimes he would get up early in the morning while it was still dark and sneak away to pray (Mark 1:35). At other times, he prayed deep into the night (Matt. 14:23). Often these times of prayer and solitude precede or follow great works or important teachings. Jesus understood the principle of recovery.

For Jesus, rhythms of work and rest included observing Sabbath customs. To him the Sabbath was not so much a duty as a delight (Mark 2:27). Jesus's times of prayer, solitude, and Sabbath rest were the very foundation of his ministry. He understood he could not do the great works that the Father was asking of him unless he first spent time alone with the Father.

Jesus's prayer in the garden of Gethsemane was more than agonizing over the cross. Through relationship with the Father in prayer, Jesus was also gaining the energy he needed to offer himself as a sacrifice. As he prayed, "My Father, if it is possible, may this cup be taken from me. Yet not as I will, but as you will" (Matt. 26:39). Jesus was simultaneously submitting to the will of the Father *and* gaining the strength to do that will. He also asked his disciples to pray that they might not fall into temptation (Matt. 26:41). Jesus knew they needed prayer to strengthen them for the coming ordeal. Unfortunately, they fell asleep instead. Do our rhythms of prayer strengthen us, or are we falling out of rhythm with Jesus?

RHYTHMS OF LIFE AND WORK

Christian leaders need to learn the lesson of the tsunami: we need healthy rhythms of work and rest. As we rest, we engage in things that restore our soul. In later chapters, we will explore these restorative spiritual rhythms. For now, take some time to reflect on the rhythms of your life and work. Use the list of questions from earlier in this chapter as a starting point. If you want to recover from burnout, you need to know how your rhythms (or lack thereof) are contributing to the problem. Share your reflections with a safe friend, a mentor, or a trained professional who can ask clarifying questions to help you go a little deeper than you would on your own.

1. In what ways are you a tsunami leader or a healthy leader?
2. If your life is like the waves in the ocean, what are the peaks and troughs you can identify in your days, weeks, months, and years?

3. Do you consider your work a sprint or a marathon? What types of recovery do you need to do your best work?

4. In God's presence, meditate on Jesus's rhythms of prayer, solitude, and Sabbath rest. What do you feel the Holy Spirit calling you to change?

PART 2

RECOVERING FROM BURNOUT

6

RECONNECTING

B ryce had a dream of becoming a Navy SEAL—a member of the
elite special forces unit who are masters of combat on sea, air,
and land. For two months, he trained his body and mind for
peak performance in swimming, running, injury prevention, nutrition, mental toughness, and the basics of military life. He passed the
Naval Special Warfare Preparatory School in Great Lakes, Illinois.
This school's goal is to improve a SEAL candidate's readiness for
the grueling trials of BUD/S[1]—the six-month training necessary to
become a Navy SEAL. Bryce was ready.

BUD/S began with a three-week orientation where Bryce became
familiar with the obstacle course, practiced swimming, and learned
the values of teamwork and perseverance. Along with the other candidates, Bryce had to demonstrate character, integrity, and a passion
for excellence. Only then would he be allowed to start the first of
three BUD/S phases.

Phase one is the toughest, consisting of eight weeks of basic
conditioning, with "Hell Week"—a torturous tool used to filter out
candidates—right in the middle. Even though months of training

remain after Hell Week, if a candidate makes it over that hurdle, he or she will most likely become a Navy SEAL.

Hell Week is a test of physical endurance, mental tenacity, and true teamwork. Each candidate is pushed to the breaking point, forcing them to make the one choice they all face: quit by ringing a bell at the center of camp or push beyond their perceived limit to find another level of mental and physical strength. They endure physical pain, miserable wet-cold conditions approaching hypothermia, deep fatigue, and sleep deprivation. Every candidate questions their core values, motivations, and limits—everything they are made of and stand for. More than two-thirds of Bryce's class "rang the bell." Those who gritted it out to the finish would hear their instructors yell the longed-for words, "Hell Week is secured!"

Bryce was almost there. He was a few hundred yards from finishing the last test of the hardest week of his life. That's when Bryce "hit the wall." His body refused to go any farther. He tried to will himself to keep going, but his limbs would not obey. He didn't want to give up, but the strength of his arms and legs abandoned him. In the icy water, his body was shutting down. With nothing more to give, he was going to drown. Should he quit and cry out for help or die trying to achieve his dream?[2]

RINGING THE BELL

Many leaders make the mistake of thinking they can work their way out of burnout. They tell themselves, "I got myself into this mess, and I can get myself out." They try harder, schedule more, and look for new strategies. None of it works. Then they hit the wall, that point when we reach the end of ourselves and have nothing left to give. Like Bryce drowning in the icy waters, we wonder if we should ring the bell and quit—quit trying, quit working, quit life. The desperation of this moment is terrifying. Leaders can make drastic mistakes or tragic choices when they realize they have nothing left to give.

The biggest mistake leaders make when they are in burnout is trying to get through it alone. Please hear me: *you cannot fully recover from burnout without help.* You may be able to get back on your feet for a while by taking a vacation or making some changes, but eventually you will burn out again. To recover fully, you need at least one objective person to help you uncover the ways you have lied to yourself. You need someone in your corner helping you face reality with brutal honesty and courage.

When Bryce found himself beginning to sink into the cold water, what was missing? He had put in the years of physical and mental training. He had passed the preparatory school. He even made it through 99 percent of Hell Week. Recounting Bryce's story, author Henry Cloud says Bryce found strength in the encouragement of a fellow candidate named Mark.

> As he told the story of going down, about to call for help and signal that it was over for him, his eyes fell upon the land ahead. There was Mark, standing on the shore. Mark saw him, and Bryce said that Mark gave him a huge fist pump and a yell, signaling to Bryce that "he could do it." Their eyes locked for a few seconds, and as Bryce described it, something happened. Something beyond him. His body jumped into another gear, into another dimension of performance that he had not had access to before; he was able to get back on top of the cold water again and swim toward the finish line. He made it. He finished. He would be a SEAL.[3]

To recover from burnout, you will need help. Rather than ringing the bell and quitting, you can find the courage and freedom to heal through the support of another person. But to do that, you will need to step out of isolation and into relationship. You will need to reconnect with yourself and with leaders who know this terrain. As you begin the work of overcoming burnout, you will need to find relationships that help you heal and grow into a new way of leading. Whenever I talk to burned-out leaders, I recommend that they reconnect with friends who are encouraging and safe people. I direct them to find a mentor, and I also steer them toward several professionals who can help, including a physician, a coach, a counselor, and a spiritual director.

ENDING ISOLATION

When I hit the wall, I knew I needed help to understand what was happening. So I started looking for guides to help me navigate the burnout terrain. At that time, I didn't know of anyone who had recovered from burnout, so I began by searching online. After reading a few small articles that told me I wasn't alone but didn't offer much help, I stumbled upon a book by Wayne Cordeiro called *Leading on Empty*. Reading Cordeiro's story, I began to see how my people-pleasing tendencies, self-deception, and desire for affirmation were fueling my burnout. I also discovered a whole world of books by leaders who had faced burnout. I felt like I was part of a secret club, but that was part of the problem: my attempt to recover from burnout was secret. I compulsively devoured books about burnout, leadership, and soul care. However, I wasn't connecting with anyone who could look me in the eye and ask hard questions. I needed friends.

Friends

The television show *Dangerous Grounds* focused on coffee connoisseur Todd Carmichael as he searched the globe for new sources of locally grown, premium coffee beans. Todd traveled to potentially dangerous countries where he didn't know anyone. While watching the show one night, I had an epiphany. Whenever Todd found a region that grew the coffee he was looking for, he would walk up to a stranger and say, "I need a friend. Will you help me?" This led to a new relationship that enabled Todd to accomplish his goal: buying great coffee directly from the growers at a fair price.

I'm sure many of Todd's interactions were staged for the cameras, but something inside me clicked when he said, "I need a friend." *That's what I need too!* A friend to help me through the dangerous territory of burnout. So I started connecting with people who would love me without trying to fix me, people who would support me while allowing me to struggle and heal at my own pace.

The local ministerial association was a great place to connect with other pastors of different denominations. We met for lunch twice a month simply to encourage one another. While all the pastors in this group became good friends, I found deeper friendship with Jesse, a new pastor who asked my advice from time to time. We started meeting occasionally to talk about theology, which was a common interest. We went to conferences together and became close. Jesse's friendship gave me a safe space outside my own leadership problems.

If you are in burnout, true friends are refreshing. However, it's important that these friends are safe people. Unsafe people will drain you further through judgment, giving advice, and other attempts to fix you. A true friend will respect you as a person and come alongside you as an equal. They won't look down on you but will lift you up in a way that feels affirming, energizing, and inspiring.

A quick note just for pastors: There's a debate in ministry circles about whether it's safe to develop friendships with people in the church you serve. Some say no, that making friends with people in your church compromises your ability to pastor them well. However, it is possible to be both a pastor and a friend if you keep the roles distinct and maintain clear boundaries. Some pastors avoid friendships within the church because they are afraid of getting burned. These pastors are more likely to become isolated and burn out, especially in rural churches.

Developing friendships among other pastors is crucial, but it can present problems too. Pastors who are struggling may be reluctant to develop friendships within their own denomination because they are afraid that if they admit any difficulty, it could affect a future call. Pastors in your community may see you as a threat or competition. Don't let these fears keep you from pursuing healthy friendships within the church, in your community, and among your peers. Like all friendships, it's important to choose safe, loving people. Friends like this will make you far less likely to burn out.

Mentor

I also reached out to a fellow pastor from a nearby town. This guy was completely different from me. I'm introverted, quiet, and reserved. He's extroverted, bold, and outspoken. We had differences in theology, differences in politics, and we were in very different leadership roles. Our only common ground was that we pastored churches in the same area, and we had both been to India on a mission trip. Ten years earlier, we had met for lunch once to talk about our shared experience in India. That was the only real conversation we ever had until I reached out to him via email and asked if we could talk.

Dave McMahon agreed to become my mentor. We met for breakfast every Thursday, and for that first year, Dave wouldn't even let me pay for my meal. He took me to the Pastor's Conference at Moody Bible Institute in Chicago. While there, he treated me to deep dish pizza, Italian beef sandwiches, and other culinary favorites. We talked about my struggles in ministry, and most of the time, he just listened and commiserated with me. He didn't offer advice unless I asked for it. Mostly, he helped me see that I wasn't alone and that my experience was not unusual. While I never adopted Dave's larger-than-life personality, his friendship helped me to become more comfortable with myself and my true leadership style. His gracious presence enabled me to find the courage to ask for help more often.

A good mentor is someone with experience in your field who wants to see you succeed. They can identify with your struggles and are respectful in the way they offer advice or correction. When they have hard things to say, they don't hold back but affirm that they are in your corner and have your best interests in mind. They ask you difficult questions and challenge your assumptions without making you feel slighted or diminished.

Doctor

A doctor who is patient and willing to listen is truly a gift. Dr. Marshall Wickens was such a gift to me. When I consulted him about my stress and burnout, he told me I needed to take a break—for as long as I could. I needed rest and a new perspective, and that couldn't happen while I was working in a stress-filled environment. We talked about how my physical health could be contributing to my fatigue. He ordered blood tests to check for conditions that would drain my energy. Eventually, we decided that my burnout was not caused by physical problems, although losing some weight wouldn't hurt. He suggested an antianxiety medication, which I unwisely refused. As we talked about my physical condition, Dr. Wickens also offered encouragement and a calm presence that gave me hope.

Your primary care doctor can help you determine if there are physiological causes behind your burnout. Depression, fatigue, and anxiety can originate entirely within the body. For example, someone with undiagnosed celiac disease will feel deep fatigue and maybe even depression. High levels of certain hormones can lead to feelings of constant anxiety. At the very least, go get a physical and be honest with your doctor about how you feel. Ask them to test for any physical causes for your burnout symptoms.

Coach

I was listening to the *200churches* podcast when hosts Jeff and Jonny interviewed Dave Jacobs, a ministry coach. I didn't even know there were coaches for pastors, but I found Dave's website and contacted him to set up some coaching. He asked great questions to help me clarify my issues and affirmed I was moving in the right direction. Talking with an impartial third party was so beneficial. After about four months of coaching, I had confidence that I was on the right track and could move forward on my own. Now I coach pastors and ministry leaders through burnout.

Every leader needs a coach to help you think through issues so you can work toward the best version of you. Whether you hire a ministry coach or an executive leadership coach, having someone who can help you clarify your thinking and find the way forward is totally worth the cost. Working with a coach usually happens in seasons of need. My clients usually work with me for a few months at a time. However, I do have long-term coaching clients too. Think of this as an "as needed" relationship for times of crisis, when you feel stuck, or when you want a leadership check-up.

I've watched leaders move from "I don't know if I can do this anymore" to "I'm totally excited about the future" in as little as three months of coaching. A good coach will ask hard questions to help you get to the root of a problem, design a path forward, and encourage you along the way. He or she won't tell you what to do but will help you to discover your own solutions. You are the expert on you. A good coach will listen to your story and help you design a solution unique to you and your situation. It's up to you to do the work, but having a coach in your corner can make it so much easier.

I also tell my coaching clients, "If you are in a crisis, feel free to send up a flare and text me for a free emergency session." These aren't full one-hour sessions, but they are valuable for processing leadership pain in the moment. I direct the client by asking questions that will help them calm down, think about the situation creatively, and find hope for the immediate future. Having a calm, nonanxious presence to help you process extreme anxiety in the moment is a great way to learn the skills you need for handling future crises.[4] We will often debrief these emergency calls in our next full coaching session to glean insights.

Counselor

One of the most important relationships in my healing from burnout was my counselor. It's amazing how much of our anxiety and loss of self starts in childhood. My counselor helped me work through my present problems too, but as he asked questions, the root of some of those problems often went back to childhood feelings of inadequacy, exclusion, or abuse (bullying). As an adult, I was able to reevaluate and reframe those childhood experiences so I didn't have to carry the pain and fear any longer. A good counselor will help with more than just childhood wounds. They will help us explore our present relationships too and make plans for future relational success. Working through my perfectionism, my negative self-talk, my overresponsibility, and my people-pleasing assumptions about others helped me rediscover my true self. It took many months, but I was able to find a much healthier way of being in the world.

Make sure your counselor is a good fit for you. Look for a licensed professional counselor you can trust who makes you feel comfortable. As a Christian, I knew it would be important to find a Christian counselor who would understand and share my core beliefs. My counselor was able to use my faith as part of my healing process because he shared this same faith.

I am amazed at how many leaders refuse to go to counseling. Either they think that using a counselor is a sign of weakness or they are afraid to address their childhood wounds. Some refuse to see a counselor because they are afraid of what their followers will think. This approach is foolish. You will never be free from burnout if you don't take the time to explore how your past influences your current thinking. Unless those past wounds are acknowledged, you will never be free of anxiety in the present.

Please find the courage to see a licensed professional counselor for six months or more. If you cannot afford counseling, don't be afraid to ask about a sliding scale based on your income. Many counselors even offer a limited number of pro bono slots. Counseling is especially important if you suffered trauma or abuse in the past. Your burnout may be those wounds begging to be healed, so be sure to see a trauma counselor as these issues require a trauma-informed approach.

Spiritual Director

As a Christian and as a pastor, I knew I needed to understand what the Holy Spirit was saying to me through my burnout. Part of my recovery was reading Sharon Garlough Brown's *Sensible Shoes* series. In those works of spiritually formative fiction, I connected with the character of Hannah, a pastor working through burnout and walking a similar path to mine. In the first novel, Hannah begins to see a spiritual director. As I read about these encounters, I knew this type of relationship was exactly what I needed. So I reached out to Sharon and asked if she could recommend a spiritual director for me.

Since that time, I've met with three different spiritual directors, each of whom has helped me find a deeper, more personal relationship with God. Barbara Peacock says, "Spiritual direction is the practice of discerning the activity of God in the life of another."[5] A spiritual director is someone who listens to your story and hears the deeper spiritual movements in it. William Barry and William Connolly define spiritual direction as "help given by one believer to another that enables the latter to pay attention to God's personal communication to him or her, to respond to this personally communicating God, to grow in intimacy with this God, and to live out the consequences of the relationship."[6] They help you see and respond in appropriate ways to the Holy Spirit's leading.

Ruth Haley Barton's spiritual director once told her, "Ruth, you are like a jar of river water all shaken up. What you need is to sit still long enough so that the sediment can settle and the water can become clear."[7] My spiritual directors have provided space and time for me to be still before God. This posture of stillness, silence, and waiting on God is just what I need for my soul to settle. Henri Nouwen says, "Those who have really listened to God's voice have often found themselves being called away from familiar and relatively comfortable places to places they would rather not go."[8] According to Barbara Peacock, spiritual direction helped Dr. Martin Luther King Jr. find this type of clarity and courage to lead the civil rights movement.[9]

Please don't ignore the spiritual aspects of your burnout. Your spirit connects with your body, mind, will, and emotions as a unified whole. If you are to be free from the disconnected, disintegrated way of being, you will need to explore your spiritual life. I believe that the only way to find complete wholeness is through a relationship with Jesus as he is described in the Bible.

Spiritual direction isn't for everyone, but if you find yourself wanting more out of your spiritual life, or if you are craving silence and solitude but don't know where to begin, a spiritual director might be what you need. Before committing yourself to the care of a spiritual director, ask questions to make sure that they are trained and certified and that their approach and beliefs are in line with your faith. Warning: working with a spiritual director may introduce some healthy disruption into your life.

HOW TO FIND SAFE PEOPLE

If there's one thing I want you to remember from this chapter, it's this: *you can't face burnout alone.* You need safe people in your life who can help you express and process your pain, anxiety, and frustration.

If you're in burnout, you're probably experiencing some relational conflict, and I know it's hard to trust anyone at such times. The six relationships listed above can help you begin that journey of trust. I needed all six relationships at once, but you may only need two or three (though I hope you can see how you would benefit from all six). However, you don't need to hire professionals to find safe relationships. There are traits to look for in others that will help you develop a group of trustworthy people who can refuel your spirit. In the book *People Fuel*, John Townsend lists twenty-two characteristics of people who will help you refuel, and he breaks them into four main categories. I use this list as a guide for who I want to be as a ministry coach and friend.[10]

1. **SAFE PEOPLE ARE PRESENT WITH YOU.** They will accept you, validate your experience, respond to your feelings, and listen with empathy. They will provide comfort and support, and they won't be disturbed by your strong emotional responses.

2. **SAFE PEOPLE HELP YOU SEE THE GOOD.** They will affirm and encourage you truthfully. They will respect you and offer hope. They are forgiving and grace-filled people. They will pause to ensure that you see the wins and will celebrate these wins with you.

3. **SAFE PEOPLE WILL HELP YOU SEE REALITY.** They will ask questions for clarification and offer different perspectives and insights that deepen your understanding. They will give feedback but usually only when you ask for it. They will ask hard questions and confront you when needed.

4. **SAFE PEOPLE WILL CALL YOU TO ACTION.** They will offer advice when asked. They will help you find structure and challenge you to grow. They create an environment where you can flourish, and they won't be satisfied with the status quo. They will lead you to serve others.

These are the type of people you want to seek out. While one person may not possess all these characteristics, you should make sure they have a good number of them before entrusting yourself fully to them. The goal is to find people with whom you can be completely open without fear. Make a list of people in your life who match each characteristic. You may be surprised to find you have more trustworthy friends than you thought. These names are a good place to start, but take it slow and risk trust in small steps. As a person proves trustworthy, you can open up more of yourself to them.

In the next chapter we will begin the work of restoring your true self. However, your first step to overcoming burnout is to build a team of safe people who can help you through the growth process. A team that includes safe friends and qualified professionals will give you the best foundation for future health. Here are some questions to help you build a good support network:

1. Who are the people closest to you? Which of them deserve to know what you are going through? How will you tell them about the way you feel?

2. Using the descriptions of safe people from this chapter, which of your friends or family are in that category? How can you safely risk trust with others who show potential to be safe people?

3. Write a short description of how you feel that you can share with your doctor. Be sure to share how you feel physically, mentally, and emotionally because they are all interconnected.

4. Do you know someone who would be a good mentor? Ask them if they would be willing to meet you for coffee or a meal. At that meeting, how will you ask them for help?

5. Start doing some research on good therapists in your area or who will meet with you online. Create a list of licensed

professional counselors that you can call when you are ready. (If you're a pastor, pirministries.org can help you find a good counselor. Others may want to look to betterhelp. com or a similar service that will find and vet counselors.)

6. Explore the leadership coaching options for your field. What will it cost to hire a coach? I recommend meeting with a coach twice per month for at least three to six months and once per month after that until you are free from burnout. List potential coaches and ask them if they will give you a free first session to see if they are a good fit.

7. What are your thoughts about spiritual direction? If it sounds like something you need, start by researching spiritual directors in your faith tradition. What are your must-have qualities in a spiritual director?

7

RESTORATION
OF SELF

When I was fifteen, I bought a silly pin-on button that read:

> *I've gone off to find myself.*
> *If I return before I get back,*
> *please tell me to wait.*

Burnout recovery has similarities to the confusion and self-discovery of the teenage years. It feels disorienting, as many of our previously held beliefs about God, self, and others prove to be ineffective and unreliable. The burnout cycle won't stop until we find a more reliable self—one that relates to God and others in truth and love. So that the true self can emerge, the false self must be exposed as an imposter. We're on a journey to find ourselves, and we don't know what to expect. It's an adventure!

Your sense of self started to form in childhood. As you watched and learned from your parents, you began to mimic their ways of walking, talking, and being in the world. Your identity was wrapped up in who they were and what they expected of you. Soon other people became role models as well—grandparents, teachers, coaches, and peers all influenced the way you behaved and how you understood yourself. Many of those relationships were good and healthy, but everyone experiences unhealthy (even dangerous) interactions from time to time. During these times we develop defense mechanisms to keep ourselves safe.

These defensive postures and learned behaviors combine to form a false self that we project to the world. It's not false in the sense that we are intentionally lying, but rather it's not a true representation of self—it's what we think we need to be to receive love and acceptance from others. This idea of false self and true self shows up in modern psychology, but it has its roots in the Christian contemplative tradition (like *The Interior Castle* by Teresa of Ávila). What is the false self? David Benner says, "At the core of the false self is a desire to preserve an image of our self and a way of relating to the world. This is our personal style—how we think of ourselves and how we want others to see us and think of us."[1]

In the Disney movie *Encanto*, the Madrigal family has wonderful magical gifts that benefit the community. These amazing gifts provide abilities far beyond normal human capacity, like superhuman strength, emotions that control the weather, meals that heal, and incredible hearing. However, there is one gift that the family doesn't appreciate. Bruno has the ability to see glimpses of the future. When his visions foretell something bad, Bruno goes into hiding, and the rest of the family acts as if he never existed, leading to the popular song "We Don't Talk About Bruno." He becomes the black sheep of the family Madrigal.

Many families don't talk about the bad stuff. As a child you may have learned that if you pointed out something that was painful or potentially embarrassing to the family, your parents or siblings would get angry. To avoid their wrath, you learned to avoid that stuff. Over time, you came to accept that in order to be loved and accepted in this family you had to ignore the painful parts of life and only focus on the good. You made a childhood vow that no matter how you felt, you would acknowledge the good and happy feelings and repress the sad, angry, or other unwanted feelings. In this moment, part of your true self was being denied and your false self was emerging.

We all make childhood vows like this. First, we experience something painful, like teasing or bullying at school, an embarrassing moment, or a time we failed at something. Maybe we misunderstood an event (like thinking myopia meant I was going blind). Maybe we suffered abuse or neglect. Whatever the event, the pain of it leads us to create a defense mechanism, some way of avoiding that pain in the future. We vow to never let that happen again. We shut down emotionally, withdraw from relationships, or present an aggressive or angry front to the world. The defenses we create become rules or scripts we live by.

For a while, the vows we make in our childhood and teen years protect us and help us to understand the world. As we enter adulthood, however, they start to get in the way of healthy relationships. For example, my vow to not trust people was helpful at first, but eventually it created a barrier to making new friends or having long-term relationships. By the time we're adults, most of us have discovered that people—all people—will hurt us at some point. We learn to confront and forgive, and our friendships become stronger as a result. My childhood vow—along with several others that I made from being bullied, teased, and verbally abused—made me self-protective and withdrawn. How can you learn to forgive if you never let anyone get close enough to hurt you?

My first day of high school was awful. My family had just moved to a new city, so I didn't have any friends. I walked into school not knowing a single person. No one talked to me, and because of my childhood vows, I didn't take the risks necessary to make friends. I remember coming home and crying over the cruelty of a silent world. While it was never this extreme again, this pattern of isolation repeated in every new situation well into my college years. To be honest, I still struggle to risk trust whenever I am alone in a group of new people.

What are the defense mechanisms that kept you safe as a child but now get in your way? We all have them. Most of us have built our whole sense of self around pleasing others, avoiding pain, and projecting a positive image. This is what we call the *false self.* It's not who we truly are. It's a facade that we use to hide our true self so we don't get hurt. Over time it becomes the only self we know, and our true self gets lost behind our self-protective walls, defenses, and false image.

We need to rediscover who we were made to be: our *true self.* This isn't a narcissistic pursuit of self, for pride leads us away from God. No, the search for the true self is one of humility. In *Wholeheartedness,* Chuck DeGroat explains:

> As it turns out, our soul's journey to self-discovery isn't at all narcissistic. What is narcissistic is our exhausting, self-sabotaging life of perfectionism, whether we pursue it through financial success or religious ritual or even finding God's perfect match for us. . . . We're hidden to some degree—hidden behind false selves who make us strangers to our true selves, hidden behind fig-leaved garments that veil our shame and insecurity and anxiety. We're hidden, and we're exhausted. Deprived of the wholeness for which we've been made, we settle for half-lives.[2]

The key to overcoming burnout is to rediscover your true self and to walk in the humility and integrity of knowing who you truly are. To do that, you need to become whole, secure, and separate from others. These are the gifts God wants to give us if we are willing to open ourselves to his healing presence.

YOUR WHOLE SELF

As I said earlier, burnout is the condition of having your personal identity overwhelmed by the anxiety of life—a total depletion of self. Most people experiencing burnout have compartmentalized their lives (see chapter 3). To recover, that fragmented self needs to be healed and brought back to God's original design of a unified, whole self. Genesis 2:7 says, "The Lord God formed man of the dust of the ground, and breathed into his nostrils the breath of life; and man became a living soul" (KJV). This text contains one of the most important truths from Scripture for your recovery: you are a unified self, created in God's image. If we are to live with integrity, then we must rediscover and understand this principle.

Notice how Genesis 2:7 describes the creation of the first human. First, God forms a body from the dust of the ground. Next, he breathes into him the breath of life. No matter how one interprets the creation narrative, a fundamental principle within the Christian tradition is that as human beings we are created by God with both body and spirit (or breath of life). Pastors sometimes debate how many parts there are to a human being (body, spirit, soul, etc.). In this text, however, we see God creating the body and breathing into it a life-giving principle (the spirit). When God does this, we are told that man becomes a living being. The word that most modern Bible versions translate as "being" is rendered as "soul" in the King James Version. In Hebrew, it's the word *nephesh*, which can mean "soul" or "self."[3] So when God joins the spirit to the body, the man becomes a unified self. *As a human being, you are created to be a unified self.* But because of sin, we have fractured ourselves into pieces. Ultimately, after the resurrection, in the new heaven and new earth, this unified self will be fully and truly restored.

Part of the gospel message is that through Jesus we can become whole again, but for that to happen we need a new heart. Proverbs 4:23 says, "Above all else, guard your heart, for everything you do flows from it." Our speech, actions, will, and attitudes flow from the heart, which is the core of our self. In Scripture the phrase "hardness of heart" is a way of describing our sinfulness. We act out of a heart that is hard toward God and his ways. The message of the gospel is that God can and will give us a new heart. In Hebrews 8:10, God promises, "I will put my laws in their minds and write them on their hearts." In Ezekiel 36:26, he says, "I will give you a new heart and put a new spirit in you; I will remove from you your heart of stone and give you a heart of flesh."

Your burnout stems from living as a divided, false self. Not that burnout is sinful in itself, but this divided self is a natural response to living in a world stained by sin and influenced by the sinfulness around us (and in us). However, if you are a Christian, God has already given you a new heart that loves his law and desires to do his will. Now you must learn to live from that new way of being. Jesus said to his disciples, "Learn from me, for I am gentle and humble in heart, and you will find rest for your souls" (Matt. 11:29).

Following Jesus and learning his ways will help us to live from the new heart that God has given us by his Holy Spirit. What motivates Jesus? What are his values and priorities? What does his heart love? Jesus followed God, his Father. In the gospel of John, he describes himself as deriving energy from doing the Father's will and fulfilling his work.[4] Jesus spoke what the Father told him to say[5] and did what he saw the Father doing.[6] Jesus is a flesh and blood image of the Father—doing the Father's will, speaking the Father's words, and following the Father's example. This is what it means to be the image of God: to follow God from a pure heart.

In Genesis 1:26–28 we read,

> Then God said, "Let us make mankind in our image, in our likeness, so that they may rule over the fish in the sea and the birds in the sky, over the livestock and all the wild animals, and over all the creatures that move along the ground."

So God created mankind in his own image,
    in the image of God he created them;
    male and female he created them.

God blessed them and said to them, "Be fruitful and increase
in number; fill the earth and subdue it. Rule over the fish in the sea
and the birds in the sky and over every living creature that moves
on the ground."

God created humankind in his image and charged them to fill
the earth, to bring order to it, and to rule over it. God himself was
doing these same things earlier in the chapter. In Genesis 1:2 we read,
"Now the earth was formless and empty, darkness was over the surface of the deep, and the Spirit of God was hovering over the waters."
This verse presents three problems: (1) the earth was formless or chaotic, (2) the earth was empty, and (3) the earth was dark.

God brings order out of chaos by separating light from dark and
water from land. He fills the earth with plants and animals so that it will
no longer be empty. He creates the sun to rule the day and the moon
to rule the night. God solves the problems of Genesis 1:2 by bringing
order, filling the earth, and establishing rule. Then he creates humans,
male and female, in his image—to continue his work of bringing order,
filling the earth, and ruling over it. In the context of Genesis 1, being
made in the image of God means following God's example and doing
God's will. This is exactly what we see Jesus doing in the Gospels. Jesus
is showing us how to live as someone made in the image of God. He
teaches us how to be whole again, how to live as our true self.

YOUR BROKEN SELF

To live as a unified, whole person, we need to start identifying the
ways our sinful, selfish false self has led us to reject both God and

our true self that is made in God's image. We must identify how we have become disordered, empty, and chaotic in our souls. In Romans 1:18–32, the apostle Paul describes how we have exchanged the truth for a lie, leading to disordered hearts, empty passions, and chaotic minds. Paul says that we suppress the truth by our wickedness and that we have exchanged the truth about God for a lie (Rom. 1:18–25).

Sin begins with a lie. We usually think of sin as violating a list of dos and don'ts. We believe that when we steal we have sinned because we violated God's command "You must not steal." However, theft is really a *symptom* of sin in the same way a fever and cough are symptoms of a virus. Stealing is the result of not believing God and not trusting him to provide. We are not righteous but sinful; therefore, we suppress what we know to be God's truth and substitute our own lie in its place. Humans have been doing this since the fall in Genesis 3.

In the garden, Eve (and Adam with her) disregarded God's command "You must not eat from the tree of the knowledge of good and evil, for when you eat from it you will certainly die" (Gen. 2:16–17). Instead, she listened to the serpent's question "Did God really say . . . ?" and his reasoning "God knows that when you eat from it your eyes will be opened, and you will be like God," (Gen 3:4–5). The classic lie of all sin is "You will be like God." Adam and Eve believed the lie and ate the fruit.

Notice how Eve exchanges the truth of God for a lie. The truth was "For when you eat from it you will certainly die." She discards that truth and replaces it with "The fruit of the tree was good for food and pleasing to the eye, and also desirable for gaining wisdom." The tree is death, and she calls it life. Her sin isn't in the eating; that action is the fruit of the lie. Her sin is that she called God a liar in her heart. Don't put all the blame on Eve though. Adam, by his actions, agreed with Eve, as have we all ever since.

All sin starts with the attitude that we can be like God or that we know better than he does. We suppress the truth then exchange it for a lie. Our whole lives we have lived this way. In our minds we have dethroned God and put ourselves in his place. This has consequences for how we relate to our world. Paul fleshes this out in Romans 1 by showing how we have disordered hearts, empty passions, and chaotic minds.

Disordered Hearts

The first consequence of exchanging the truth of God for a lie is that God gives us up to disordered hearts (Rom. 1:24–25). "God gave them up" means that God allowed us to have our sinful desires and the consequences that come with them. Paul uses the phrase "desires of their hearts" (CSB) to describe how we have become controlling. In Western culture, the word *heart* typically refers to one's emotions. We connect the heart to things like nervous energy, fear, love, and loss. "She wears her heart on her sleeve." "He was so afraid that he lost all heart." "My heart is broken; how can I go on without him?"

The Bible uses the word *heart* somewhat differently to convey the very core of a person—that is, the self. The heart contains the mind, will, emotions, and personality—everything that makes you *you*. The heart can think (Ps. 16:7), choose (Prov. 23:15), feel (Prov. 15:13), scheme (Prov. 6:18), and express itself (Ps. 57:7). So when Paul refers to the "lusts of their hearts," he is saying that the whole self has become disordered or disintegrated. By suppressing God's truth and elevating our own lies, we have lost our true selves. Something is missing, and that something is the real us.

Empty Passions

Not only have we lost our true selves, but we have also lost our true love. Romans 1:26 says that God gave us up to "dishonorable passions" (ESV)—that is, passions that are empty of honorable purpose. Instead of giving genuine love that seeks the other's best good (God first, then neighbor), we take for ourselves what the world calls "love" through sex, manipulation, or other expressions of power.

One example is how lust has disordered sexual intercourse. God designed sex as the joining of two into one. It's intended to be the giving of one's self for the fulfilment of another, a truly selfless act. Now sex has become something we take to fill our own wants. We have lost all sense of "the other," and people become objects for our taking. We use one another for self-gratification, and even if it's consensual, it isn't love. Instead of filling through self-giving intimacy, we empty one another through lustful greed.

We see this in other areas of life too. At work we use others to get ahead or to make a profit. We use our kids to fulfill our own unmet dreams or to prop up our low self-esteem.

This is also true in our loving relationship with God. We no longer worship him as worthy of adoration, service, and love. We no longer live for his glory or to reveal his greatness. Think about how you pray. Is it to get God to do what you want him to do or to submit to what God's wants in your life? We are designed to want God's kingdom to come and God's will to be done. Instead, we try to make God serve our needs, and when that doesn't work, we make gods of wood, metal, and stone to serve us. We no longer connect with God and others in healthy ways. When we lose our self, we lose everyone else too! No wonder we feel so empty.

Chaotic Minds

Our reasoning cannot be pure and right if we are going to maintain life based on a lie. Because we did not acknowledge God, Paul says that God gave us over to a "depraved mind" (Rom. 1:28). The result of this is that we have turned everything upside down. Look at how Paul describes the change in verse 32: "Although they know God's righteous decree that those who do such things deserve death, they not only continue to do these very things but also approve of those who practice them." We have chosen death over life. It's chaos!

Have you ever tried to maintain a lie? The longer it goes on, the more effort is needed to keep it going. There's a part of us that is living in the lie. Then there's a part of us that is living out of what we think is true. And there's a third part that is doing everything in our power to keep the other two parts from meeting. We divide ourselves up into little pieces and then wonder why we can't keep things straight.

YOUR RESTORED SELF

The presence of the Holy Spirit within us is the unifying force of our lives. He takes what we've shattered and brings wholeness to our souls once again. This doesn't happen all at once, but we can see it over time. If you are going to recover from burnout, you will need the healing power of the Spirit to help you identify the shattered pieces within you. Alison Cook and Kimberly Miller, in their book *Boundaries for Your Soul*, use the framework of internal family systems to help us understand how this is possible. They identify three key parts within each of us: the parts that try to protect us from pain (which they call *managers* and *firefighters*) and the wounded or broken parts (called *exiles*). The key to healing and unifying these parts is to become a *Spirit-led self*:

> Your Spirit-led self "holds you together in truth." From here you can draw a troubling emotion in closer or ask it to step back, so you can develop perspective. You can invite Jesus to be with the parts of you most in need of his presence. Your Spirit-led self can minister to your troubling thoughts and feelings so that they are witnessed and transformed.[7]

You will know when you are living from your Spirit-led self when you're manifesting the fruit of the Spirit: love, joy, peace, patience, kindness, goodness, faithfulness, gentleness, and self-control

(Gal. 5:22–23). When these are the primary ways you act toward yourself, you will have the following qualities:[8] calmness, clarity, curiosity, compassion, confidence, courage, creativity, and connectedness.

As the life of the Spirit within unifies our souls, we find that all the parts of us become further integrated. We begin to discover our true self—the one with the new heart—that desires to do God's will instead of being self-willed. We come into greater awareness, regulation, and healthy expression of our emotions. We no longer need to exile unwanted emotions but learn that they are a way God is speaking to us for our healing. When we are a Spirit-led self, we are finally able to be honest with ourselves and others about how we feel. We don't have to be afraid of our emotions taking over because we are under the Spirit's control. So we can admit when we are sad, lonely, angry, or grieving because, by the Spirit's leading, these emotions are useful to our growth and maturity.

As we are able to identify, regulate, and express our emotions, we also find greater unity in our thinking. This emotional security enables us to move toward clarity and understanding without fear. Learning and growth, along with the mental shifts necessary for change, become welcome allies even when we are facing the darker parts from our past or our internal world. We can trust the Spirit to lead us through the darkness to the healing light of truth.

Even our bodies benefit from this growing unification of self. Our stress levels go down, as does our addiction to the stress hormones adrenaline and cortisol. We begin to sleep better as our anxiety level decreases. We may even want to explore exercise and nutrition as ways to care for our body because we realize that our physical health is directly connected to our emotional, mental, and spiritual health. We stop ignoring the body and start listening to its warnings as indicators that something may be wrong in our soul.

As we grow in the Spirit and are led by him, we start living with integrity—all the parts of us now working more like a single, unified whole. This process is a lifelong movement we call sanctification. It's not something we can do in a weekend, a year, or even a decade. We may see great growth over those time periods, but we will always be moving toward Christlikeness. The more we allow the Spirit to lead us, the more whole we become.

RULE FOLLOWING VERSUS REINTEGRATION

If we want to be whole selves again, we need to start living with Jesus in following the Father. Too often churches have reduced following God to keeping certain commandments or following the rules of religion. This results in feelings of guilt when we cannot live up to those standards. However, the gospel teaches us that Jesus fulfilled all these standards for us. He kept all the commandments on our behalf because we can't possibly do it on our own. Focusing on the rules of religion only leads to defeat. Instead of listing rules to follow, Jesus shows us a way of being in the world. His way is being continually aware of God's presence with us and within us, listening to God's words (through Scripture reading and prayer), and having our hearts shaped by being with God. We then live out of the reshaped hearts God has given us. That's how we rediscover our whole self, our Spirit-led self.

If you find yourself asking, "What if I don't want to do the will of God?" then either the task at hand isn't really God's will, or you aren't really living from the new heart he has given you. Knowing which one it is takes discernment and practice that only come in living from a place of security in Christ.

Sin causes us to disintegrate the self that God created in his image. A major portion of recovery from burnout requires that we become a more integrated self. Take some time to meditate on what it means to be a unified, whole self—body, mind, emotions, spirit, all inseparable and interconnected.

1. Does your body feel disconnected, numb, or separate from your inner self? Have you disconnected emotionally or shut down spiritually? What parts of you feel most disconnected from the whole?

2. How do you see your shattered self (disordered heart, empty passions, and chaotic mind) disrupting your relationships with God, others, and self?

3. What parts of you have become exiled or hidden away? What parts have become overly aggressive? How does the Spirit want to heal these parts?

4. How are you seeing the fruit of the Spirit manifest in your life? What would your unified, true self look like?

5. How does Jesus model a unified self?

6. What would you like to say to God about your need for wholeness?

8

BECOMING SECURE

A major factor in my burnout was fearing what people could do to me. I was afraid that they could take away my reputation, my income, and my home. I was afraid they wouldn't accept me if they knew how I struggled with doubt and how often I felt like an imposter. I lived in constant fear that my false self would be revealed for what it is. That the image I projected to protect myself from harm would be the very thing that would destroy me.

This anxiety kept me from seeing a far greater reality, one that would eventually help me face my fears. That deepest and most profound reality is this: *we are fully and permanently loved by God in Jesus Christ.*

Nothing is more true or more real than God's love for you. And if you want to overcome burnout, you must embrace this reality. I'm not talking about just mentally agreeing with the truth. I'm talking about experiencing it at the very core of your being, until the most common thing you say about yourself is "I am loved by God." God's love for you in Christ must become your core identity. This security in Christ is the answer to all our false-self illusions.

Since burnout is heavily influenced by anxiety, recovery from burnout is rooted in security. We need to know that we are safe, that ultimately nothing can harm us. This is a hard thing to accept in a fallen world. We see pain and death all around us. If that isn't enough, we are born through pain, and we spend much of our early lives learning to avoid pain.

So how do we overcome this overwhelming feeling? By embracing the deeper reality of God's love. By being "rooted and established in love," we can comprehend "how wide and long and high and deep" is God's love and "know this love that surpasses knowledge—that you may be filled to the measure of all the fullness of God" (Eph. 3:17–19). That's the aim of this chapter, to start you on your journey toward becoming rooted and grounded in love.

BELOVED IN CHRIST

Before we can explore the depths of God's love for us in Christ, we must face up to our own self-deception. As I have worked through burnout and led others through their experiences, I've found that most of us do not think we are worthy of love. We may not be that straightforward in our self-assessment or aware we believe this. However, when the layers of deception are peeled away, I almost always find at the core a leader who deep down doesn't believe he or she is worthy of love. The thing we most often tell ourselves is "I am unlovable," and when we say that, we imply that even God couldn't love us.

As we explore God's love for us in Christ, I want you to hear this: *you are worthy of love.* God is love, God made you in his image, and therefore you are lovable. Sin and shame have broken that image and our ability to love ourselves, but Jesus took our sin and shame and crucified it. His death and resurrection have proven God's love for you. "For God so loved the world that he gave his one and only Son" (John 3:16). And as Jesus said, there is no greater love than to lay down one's life for another (John 15:13).

If God loves you, then you are lovable, and that means it's okay for you to love yourself. More than that, if God loves you, then to live in truth you *must* love yourself—not with a self-centered false love but with a pure and holy love that comes from being united to Christ. Rooted in God's love and coming from being joined to Jesus, this love for self will enable you to love others again. "And you shall love the Lord your God with all your heart and with all your soul and with all your mind and with all your strength. . . . You shall love your neighbor *as yourself*" (Mark 12:30–31 ESV, emphasis added). Your ability to love others comes from knowing you are loved by God and from first loving yourself with God's love.

SECURITY IN CHRIST

The New Testament phrase "in Christ" describes the benefits and realities of being united to Christ by faith. Through his incarnation, life, death, resurrection, and never-ending life, Jesus has joined himself to us like a husband to his wife. We have become one flesh with him (Eph. 5:31–32). Too often we think of salvation not in these relational terms but in abstract terms. Marcus Peter Johnson says, "Salvation is described as a gift to be apprehended rather than the apprehension of the Giver himself . . . the offer of the very person of Christ."[1]

Because we are one with Christ, we are described as being *in* him. Notice what Scripture says about you "in Christ." You are a new creation (2 Cor. 5:17), no longer condemned (Rom. 8:1), no longer a slave to sin (Rom. 6:6), free (Rom. 8:2), made holy and right with God (1 Cor. 6:11), with Christ in death (Rom. 6:3), resurrected with Christ to live a new life (Rom. 6:4), spiritually alive and alive to God (Rom. 5:10; Eph. 2:5), one who has the life of Christ within you (Gal. 2:20), standing in God's grace (Rom. 5:2), being formed into the image of Christ (Rom. 8:29), created to do good things (Eph. 2:10), seated with Jesus in heaven (Eph. 2:6), the righteousness of God (2 Cor. 5:21), united to all other believers (Gal. 3:28), adopted as a son (Rom. 8:15), child of God (Rom. 8:16), heir with Christ (Rom. 8:17), and inseparable from God's love (Rom. 8:39).

These are all true about you if you have faith in Christ. *They are present realities.* I'm sure that as you read these statements, some of them seemed hard to accept. Maybe that's because they contain an element of "already and not yet." For example, Scripture tells us that we have been made holy (sanctified), a past action and a present reality (Heb. 10:10). However, it also tells us that we are being made holy, a future reality that has not yet been realized (Heb. 10:14). We are already holy, and we are still being made holy.

Christ has completed the work, but these statements don't *feel* true because we are still learning to live in the reality of what Christ has done. We are still learning to live as the new creations that we already are. Though our adoption is complete, we are still learning to live in the freedom that we have as sons and heirs. We are still learning to live in the love of God even though nothing can separate us from God's love.

As we look at the two sides of the "already and not yet" equation, we tend to focus on the "not yet" and deny the "already." We tell ourselves we are not yet holy, not yet free, or not yet loved. We focus on our perceived lack instead of on God's present provision. That imbalance makes liars out of us and keeps us from living in the fullness and freedom of God's love. When we focus on our lack, we become anxious and unsure. When we focus on God's provision, we become secure and stable.

ABIDING IN CHRIST

Where does our life come from? As Christian leaders, we often look for life in our work for God. We think that if we can build a bigger church or preach a powerful message or become successful in business, then we will receive praise from God and others. By placing our whole identity in what we do for God, the energy we need for life comes from meeting our own definition of success. Failing to meet these self-imposed expectations drains us of life. We lose hope, we have no energy, and we can't care for others. Sound familiar?

Jesus gives us a different way. He says,

> I am the vine; you are the branches. Whoever abides in me and I in him, he it is that bears much fruit, for apart from me you can do nothing. . . . If you abide in me, and my words abide in you, ask whatever you wish, and it will be done for you. By this my Father is glorified, that you bear much fruit and so prove to be my disciples. As the Father has loved me, so have I loved you. Abide in my love. (John 15:5, 7–9 ESV)

Jesus says that without him we can't do anything. We can't produce fruit. The word *fruit* here describes the product of a successful branch. When the branch does what it is supposed to do, it bears fruit. However, the branch cannot bear this fruit unless it *abides* in the vine. To abide means to remain or dwell in a certain place; it's where you live. Jesus is saying that unless we live in him and derive our life from him, we can't fulfill our God-given purpose. If we focus on abiding in Christ, we will naturally bear fruit. But if we focus on bearing fruit, we will disconnect from Christ, wither, and die. Our energy comes from remaining connected to Jesus.

Shanti was preoccupied with producing fruit for Jesus and it drove her ministry. She was dedicated to sharing the love of Christ with other women, especially those who had great need. The pregnant teens and single moms that she served never doubted her love for them, but over time Shanti came to resent them. You see, Shanti was so dedicated to showing the love of Christ that she neglected to receive Christ's love for herself. She was operating out of shame, trying to prove her worth to Jesus because she felt worthless in herself. She was not abiding in Christ's love for her and serving out of the overflow of his love. She was very near to burnout because she wasn't finding life in Christ first.

What's the key to living in Jesus and having his words live in us? Abiding in his love. When we are filled with Jesus's love for us, we will naturally change to become like him, loving who he loves. Our love for God the Father deepens, and he becomes our highest priority. As we grow in God's love, we begin to love others as he loves them. Thus, we fulfill the commandments to love God and love neighbor. We become just like the vine, Jesus, loving others and willingly, joyfully giving ourselves for their good. The fruit comes naturally. Jesus will produce the results he desires as his life is present in us. Jesus, not the idea of Jesus but the person of Jesus himself, becomes our new identity.

YOUR TRUE IDENTITY IS IN CHRIST

When we are filled with the love of God in Christ, we are no longer driven by fear, by a desire to please others, or by maintaining some false image of ourselves. Love and fear cannot coexist. "There is no fear in love. But perfect love drives out fear, because fear has to do with punishment. The one who fears is not made perfect in love" (1 John 4:18). When we are filled with the love of Christ, our fear-based false self melts away, and our true self naturally emerges. As our true self comes forward, we will be amazed at how much it looks like Jesus. Let's focus on how much Jesus loves us by revisiting some of our "in Christ" realities and how they can help us abide in Christ.

In Christ You Are a New Creation

> Therefore, if anyone is in Christ, the new creation has come:
> The old has gone, the new is here! (2 Cor. 5:17)

God expresses his love for us by uniting us to Christ. This is a profound mystery. We confess it as reality, but we don't understand how it happens, except that it is the work of the Holy Spirit. In joining us to Jesus, God fulfills his promises of wholeness and healing. Our sins are forgiven, and he remembers them no more. We are given new hearts that beat for God and call him Father. He heals the brokenness of our sin—our disordered hearts, empty passions, and chaotic minds.

God gives us new hearts. He restores us to our true selves. As you'll recall from the previous chapter, in Ezekiel 36:26, God promises, "I will give you a new heart and put a new spirit in you; I will remove from you your heart of stone and give you a heart of flesh." We are no longer bound by our self-focused ways. We are free to live for God as his image bearers once again because his Spirit dwells within us. We are restored to our true and first love: our Creator and Father.

Because we have new hearts, we also have new passions. We are no longer a law unto ourselves, following our lusts and treating people as objects. Instead, we love God and others from the heart. "This is how we know that we love the children of God: by loving God and carrying out his commands. In fact, this is love for God: to keep his commands. And his commands are not burdensome" (1 John 5:2–3). We are now filled with a pure love rooted in both God's love for us and his love for others. We have been set free to love who God loves. So loving our neighbors flows naturally from our new hearts.

God has also healed us from our chaotic minds. Since God has forgiven our sin, we no longer live in shame. We can embrace the truth of God again because Jesus bore all our shame and crucified it on the cross. We also love the truth of God. In fact, that truth now lives in us (2 John 2–3).

By being united to Christ in the power of the Holy Spirit, we become new people. We have new hearts that love God, our neighbors, and ourselves. We are filled not only with love but also with truth. We have been forgiven and can now step into the light of truth and watch our shame disappear as we confess our sins, which God has forgiven in Christ.

Drew was raised in a tradition that emphasized the sinfulness of our hearts but never talked about the goodness of our new hearts in Christ. He really struggled with the language of being a new creation because he didn't feel new. All he could see was his struggle to be holy because he thought that his heart could only be wicked. It took several months of revealing how he truly loved people, cared about their well-being, and wanted to help them deepen their relationship with Christ before Drew was able to begin to see the new heart the Spirit had given him.

In Christ You Are No Longer Condemned; You Are Free!

> Therefore, there is now no condemnation for those who are in Christ Jesus, because through Christ Jesus the law of the Spirit who gives life has set you free from the law of sin and death. (Rom. 8:1–2)

We freely and openly confess our sins because we are no longer condemned in Christ. I know a man who lived with hidden sin for decades. When his sin was finally discovered, he confessed the truth of what he had done. He told me, "It felt so good to finally be free. All my guilt and shame disappeared as I confessed what I had done. I no longer had to live in fear because I knew, in Christ, I am forgiven." This man still had a long way to go to demonstrate repentance to his family and friends, but he was living in the freedom of forgiveness.[2]

Our sins no longer condemn us, so we don't have to live as defeated people. Our shame does not define us anymore. Instead, we can live as victorious people who have nothing to fear because our enemy has been defeated. We are free!

The new heart and the life of the Spirit within us allow us to live as free people—no longer slaves to sin and self. We have been set free from guilt, shame, and fear. Now we are free to live lives of love because we know we are loved. We are untouchable! Nothing can separate us from God because we are in Christ. We are free to live without fear. Free to live from the love of God within us. Free to follow God's commands because we love his ways. Free to give out of the abundance of our Father's provision, knowing that he will supply our needs. Free from the criticism and belittling of others because we are secure in Christ. All our faults, all our sins, all our shame have been embraced by his love and righteousness. We are accepted in the Beloved. We are free to live as children of the King of heaven with all the rights and privileges that royalty affords (Gal. 4:1–7).

I worked with a young pastor, Micah, who was constantly trying to prove himself to his church board. He didn't realize that this behavior was making it hard for the board to trust him because he was hyping himself so much. As Micah began to understand how this was a shame-based response to his own insecurity, he was able to remind himself that, in Christ, he had nothing to prove. That his ministry needed to flow from both his gifts and his limitations. As he shared these struggles with his board, they started to see his good leadership. Micah was set free from his own hype by humbly showing his humanity. The only way he could do this was by first recognizing his own acceptance through Christ.

You Are Being Formed into the Image of Christ

> For those God foreknew he also predestined to be conformed to the image of his Son. (Rom. 8:29)

The Holy Spirit not only unites us to Christ but also uses all things to shape and mold us to be just like Jesus—not that we lose our own identity and become carbon copies but that our identity finds its fullest expression in our unity with Christ. Everything that makes us unique and separate people takes on the character of Jesus. His love, joy, peace, patience, kindness, goodness, faithfulness, gentleness, and self-control are becoming our defining characteristics too as the Holy Spirit does his work. We are being remade into the image of God as he originally designed us. The Spirit is changing our hearts—the core of who we are—to be like Jesus.

In Christ You Are a Child of God

> For those who are led by the Spirit of God are the children of God. The Spirit you received does not make you slaves, so that you live in fear again; rather, the Spirit you received brought about your adoption to sonship. And by him we cry, "*Abba*, Father." The Spirit himself testifies with our spirit that we are God's children. (Rom. 8:14–16)

The presence of the Holy Spirit within you and the heart change that he brings are signs that you are a child of God. This evidence shows that you are united to Christ, one with the Son. You are no longer outside the household of faith. Now you are not just part of the family but an heir with the firstborn son. In ancient times the firstborn son had more rights than the rest of the family. He would receive a double portion of the inheritance because he would be responsible for caring for the family after his father died. Because of this responsibility, he had greater access to the father than every other member of the household except for the mother.

The firstborn son's special position meant that he could know the father's will and be responsible for seeing it done. It meant that he had access to all of the father's resources—whatever was necessary to do his will. The son could also conduct business on the father's behalf because he carried a ring that signified the right to act in the father's name. This is what Jesus means when he says, "You may ask me for anything in my name, and I will do it." (John 14:14). "In Jesus's name, amen" is not some sort of magic phrase we can add to our prayers to get what we want. Jesus is saying that when we are acting in his name (that is, on his behalf) to do the Father's will, we will have the Father's supply. We have everything we need to accomplish what God is calling us to do when we do it God's way and according to God's timing. As children of God, heirs with Christ, we have access to the Father's supply because he loves us.

One of the great tragedies of burnout is that it can infect our families too. When I'm working with a burned-out pastor, I always inquire about their spouse. Several times a pastor's wife has shared just how unloved she feels because of conflict or neglect from the church. In those cases, I like to help her experience being a child of God again.

To do so, we open our Bibles to Psalm 131, which says, "But I have calmed and quieted myself, I am like a weaned child with its mother; like a weaned child I am content" (v. 2). I ask her to pray this prayer along with the psalmist as she remembers what it's like to hold her children in her arms—not a nursing baby but a child who wants nothing other than to be held and loved. As she remembers that feeling, I say, "Now I want you to realize that you are the child praying in the arms of your Father." This powerful meditation is something they take with them during the times they feel unloved. Lily, a pastor's wife, told me, "When I'm feeling neglected by the church, I ask one of my kids to come snuggle with me. As I am holding them and telling them how much I love them, I remember, in that moment, that God is doing the same for me and so much more!"

In Christ You Are Loved by God

For I am convinced that neither death nor life, neither angels nor demons, neither the present nor the future, nor any powers, neither height nor depth, nor anything else in all creation, will be able to separate us from the love of God that is in Christ Jesus our Lord. (Rom. 8:38–39)

One of our most basic needs as humans is the need for love and belonging. As God said in the garden, "It is not good for the man to be alone" (Gen. 2:18). However, because of sin we are separated from God and others and have become driven by the search for love. Most, if not all, of our false-self defenses are attempts to find love and belonging or to avoid rejection.

The good news of the gospel is that our search is over. Since we are united to Christ, we are fully and permanently loved. We will never experience rejection from God. More enduring and secure than the love any human father has for his child, the love of God is complete, eternal, and never fading.

God loves every part of you with a full love. He holds nothing back. Right now he loves you just as completely as he loves Jesus. His love will never end because the Father's relationship with the Son can never end; they are in an eternal loving relationship that you are now part of in Christ. This is not to say that you have become a part of the divine Trinity but that you enjoy the love that exists within the Trinity. God's love will never fade because God doesn't change. He can't be manipulated by negative emotions or circumstances. God sees the full picture all the time, and he is full of joy. His joy overflows toward his children as love.

Hesed is a special Hebrew word used in Scripture for God's love, and it's used only of God. Hesed is impossible to translate exactly because we don't have an equivalent English word, but it's usually translated as mercy, grace, kindness, love, or faithfulness. It means all those things together. I like to refer to God's hesed as his faithful covenant love. It's a love rooted in the eternal character of God.

C. S. Lewis described the love of God as something that grows over time—not that God's love changes but that our awareness of how great it is grows as we continue in relationship with God. Lewis coined the phrase "farther up and farther in" to describe how each day is better than the one before as we grow in God's love and as all our fears fade away—especially the fear of rejection.

Secure in Christ

If anyone acknowledges that Jesus is the Son of God, God
lives in them and they in God. And so we know and rely on
the love God has for us. God is love. . . . There is no fear in
love. But perfect love drives out fear, because fear has to do
with punishment. The one who fears is not made perfect in
love. We love because he first loved us. (1 John 4:15–19)

As we grow in the love of God, we become more secure. God's
love casts out fear, and we begin to live into the fullness of being
the beloved of God. Have you ever seen a child who felt completely
secure in their father's love? There is no fear, just pure joy and peace.
This is the relationship that we enjoy with God as our Father. We
have nothing to fear—not one thing. As we go deeper into the love
of God, all our worries, anxieties, doubts, and fears melt away like
illusions. As the reality of God's love becomes the only sure and fixed
point in our lives, everything else takes on new meaning, even our
grief and pain.

Remember that in Christ you are a new creation, forgiven, free,
being formed into the image of Christ, a child of God, and fully and
permanently loved by God. This is your new identity. As you start to
see yourself as God sees you instead of through the false lens created
by sin, new realities begin to take root.

First, you become secure with yourself. Instead of seeing yourself as sinful and unable to do anything good, you can now trust the
new heart you've been given that loves God and others like Jesus
does. You can appreciate the gifts you've been given to glorify God
by blessing others and live into this special expression of your unity
with Christ.

You also begin loving yourself as God loves you. If the love of
God for us in Christ has become our new reality and identity, then
we start relating to our self with that same love. We no longer live

in the lie that we are worthless, unlovable, rejected, or needy. God's love for us makes us worthy, loved, accepted, and secure in Christ.

Luis's parents wanted him to escape poverty, so they pushed him to excellence. He loved that about them but also acknowledged the dark side of his drive to excel: no matter what he did, it was never enough. This attitude turned inward too. Luis felt like he was never good enough, smart enough, strong enough, or successful enough. As he struggled with anxiety and perfectionism, Luis was rejecting himself. Now he is learning that God's love for him means that Luis never has to be more than he is. "Good enough" has become a spiritual phrase for him. It means that he can do his best and trust God to provide for, protect, and accept him just as he is. He doesn't have to be perfect. "Just be Luis," he says.

God's faithful covenant love teaches us that God is compassionate and gracious toward us, not counting our sins against us but seeing us as his sons in Christ. Therefore, we can begin to learn how to be compassionate and gracious toward ourselves. We no longer have to listen to our negative self-talk or try to be perfect to be accepted. We are already accepted and beloved by God. We can start accepting ourselves the way God accepts us—just as we are. We can forgive ourselves because we are forgiven by God. We can look at ourselves with hope instead of despair, knowing that the Holy Spirit is using all things—even burnout—to make us like Jesus.

We are secure in God's love, and this newfound security also gives us freedom from self. We no longer have to live according to the false self and its self-protective ways. As we are filled with God's love, we become safe for others. We no longer use others for our purposes. When we are living from the love of God, we are willing to make sacrifices for the good of others, which in turn brings us joy. We even begin to love our enemies with empathy, compassion, and grace. We can forgive those who have wronged us because we ourselves have been forgiven.[3] We are able to accept the confession of others as they learn to live out their repentance by changing their ways.

Living in the love of God also means that we can have courage with others. We can come together to do the will of God in the face of opposition. The early church prayed for boldness in Acts 4, and we can encourage one another in the love of God. We can remind each other that we are accepted in Christ and that God will supply what we need to do his will. We can encourage one another that even in death, we find life through the resurrection of Christ. Not even death can separate us from the love of God in Christ Jesus.

FROM ANXIOUS TO SECURE

In the next chapter we will explore how the love of God leads us to care for our own souls. Do you know and feel that you are fully and permanently loved by God? Look back over this chapter and meditate on the Scripture passages that talk about what it means to be in Christ. To meditate means taking the truth of these passages into your heart until they become a part of you.

1. On a scale of one to ten, how fully do you live into God's love for you in Christ Jesus?
2. What can you do to make the reality of God's love a deeper part of you?
3. In what ways can you see evidence of the Holy Spirit within you? How has your heart changed to be more like Jesus?
4. How does the faithful covenant love of God (*hesed*) make you feel more secure?
5. How do you need to change the way that you relate to yourself to be more in line with God's love for you?
6. In what ways has God's love set you free to love others? How do you need to live into God's love for others more fully?

9

DIFFERENTIATION OF SELF

When we lose our sense of self in leadership, other people's opinions become our identity. We become overly attached to others and their ideas of us. Their words, feelings, and reactions form our false self. We usually come to hate this false self, but we may not understand why we feel so angry, depressed, or frustrated. We hate what others say about us because we intuitively know it doesn't reflect our true self, while at the same time we may not even know this true self. In previous chapters, we explored how to be a whole person and how to be secure in God's love are part of the work of rediscovering our true self. In these next few chapters, we will explore some steps toward becoming a separate, healthy self through a process called *differentiation of self*.

One of the big problems contributing to my burnout was people pleasing. For so many years, I didn't realize that when people criticize a pastor, it's often not really about the pastor—it's often an expression of frustration, anger, or sadness about things that are happening in their own lives. Because I didn't know this, when people pointed out a weakness of mine, I thought it was something I had to fix in myself. I

fell into a frustrating pattern of going back and forth between following my calling and trying to please others so I wouldn't be criticized.
It was exhausting, and soon I was neglecting my calling altogether.

As I was recovering from burnout, I realized that my people
pleasing was actually a lack of self-differentiation. I wasn't clear on
my own values, priorities, and boundaries. I couldn't let other people
be anxious, angry, or frustrated without it affecting my own anxiety.
As I learned to become a separate self—clear on who I am and not
infected by other people's issues—I became a more confident and
secure leader. The people pleasing was replaced with a calm, stable
presence. As Charles Stone Jr. says, "Differentiation of self is the fundamental building block for the strong leadership immune system
we need to combat people pleasing."[1]

Allow me to clarify what I mean by becoming a "separate self."
It's not about becoming completely disconnected from others.
Instead, healthy separation is about recognizing and avoiding our
tendency to blur the line between where our self ends and others
begin. Such enmeshment of self with others can lead to unhealthy
patterns. When we become too spiritually, emotionally, or psycho-
logically reliant on another person, we have become codependent.
Sometimes this shows up as a feeling of insufficiency or neediness.
Other times it's when we enable another person to continue in self-
destructive behavior because the relationship makes us feel good
about ourselves. Codependency can show up as controlling behavior
or as a willingness to be controlled. There is no separation of self
from others.

Codependent pastoral leaders have a huge need for being Mr.
Answer man or Ms. Answer woman, as well as not letting others
take responsibility for themselves. Codependent pastoral leaders have a tendency to surround themselves with excessively
needy people in hopes to become the "ONE" to care-take the

individual. Have you ever come across a pastor who has the tendency to become obsessed with and controlling of the people and problems in their environment? What about the pastor who is so preoccupied (excessively worried) with the problems or persons in the "church," so much so, that the needs of their family go unmet? Emotionally dependents, caretakers, rescuers are all names that fit the codependent pastor. What is the end result? BURNOUT!!![2]

To truly love God, we must know that we are not him. If we thought of ourselves as God, we would be violating the creature-Creator relationship. We would be dishonoring God and harming ourselves. This is the very nature of sin. Likewise, if we want to truly love our neighbor, we must be a separate person. Jesus hinted at this when he said, "Love your neighbor as yourself" (Matt. 22:39). You and your neighbor are separate people. If we do not see ourselves as separate, we violate the personhood of our neighbor. When we take responsibility for things they can and should be doing for themselves, we intrude on *their* personhood. When we expect others to do for us what we should be doing ourselves, we violate *our* own dignity.

How can you lead if you are not living as a truly separate person? Here are some common ways that we fail to self-differentiate. We might be overresponsible, taking responsibility that is not ours and rightly belongs to another. Micromanaging, hovering, and shaming people into doing something are all forms of overresponsibility. Have you ever done something just to prevent someone else from being sad or angry? When we try to manage other people's emotions, we are not living as a separate person. Letting people manipulate us into doing something we don't want to do is failing to remain separate. Giving in to whining, complaining, or the shaming of another blurs the lines between us and them.

DIFFERENTIATION OF SELF

Learning to become separate people while remaining relationally connected to others is a process that psychologist Murray Bowen called *differentiation of self*. Pastor Rich Villodas, a student of Bowen's theories, says, "Differentiation (i.e., remaining connected to people but not having your actions or reactions determined by them) is one of the greatest tasks of life. It takes a self that is anchored in God's love and growing in self-awareness to live into this."[3] This definition has at least three significant elements. First, we must remain connected to people. We can't simply cut them out of our lives so they don't affect us. (Though in cases of abusive or particularly toxic people, this may be necessary.) Second, our actions must come from within and not be determined by others. Michael Kerr and Murray Bowen describe this aspect of differentiation as a person's ability to "define his or her own life's goals and values apart from the pressures of those around them."[4] Third, we become more intentional and less reactionary. As Peter Steinke says, "Differentiation is a process in which a person moves toward a more intentional and thoughtful way of life (and a less automatic way of functioning)."[5] As we self-differentiate, we become more thoughtful and less controlled by our emotions, more intentional and less reactive to the anxiety around us.

The work we have already done toward becoming whole and secure will carry us a long way toward becoming differentiated. However, we still have several steps to become a healthy, separate individual so we can be fully present and available to others. Being fully present to others respects their individual personhood and allows us to develop deeper, healthier relationships. Before we explore how to develop differentiation of self, let's first ask, "What happens when we fail to self-differentiate?"

Failure to Self-Differentiate

When we fail to develop healthy separation from others, we become needy. Have you ever met someone that wants validation from others so much that they are unable to act without it? This is an extreme example of a poorly differentiated person. It's common to see in families with a domineering parent or in organizations with a narcissistic leader. Peter Scazzero describes such a leader:

> They need continual affirmation and validation from others because they don't have a clear sense of who they are. They depend on what other people think and feel in order to have a sense of their own worth and identity. Or out of fear of getting too close to someone and thus swallowed up, they may avoid closeness to others completely. Under stress they have little ability to distinguish between their feelings and thought (intellectual) process.[6]

It's not that these leaders are needy but that they become doormats for everyone to walk all over. Lack of healthy separation can become much more dangerous. The worst of the poorly differentiated leaders become controlling, manipulative bullies. They disregard the dignity and personhood of others and treat them as objects of their own will, like pawns on a chessboard. Think of the playground bully from your childhood. I bet he or she was someone who just wanted to be loved and accepted but didn't know how to connect with people except by fear. The Bowen Center for the Study of the Family says,

> People with a poorly differentiated "self" depend so heavily on the acceptance and approval of others that they either quickly adjust what they think, say, and do to please others or they dogmatically proclaim what others should be like and pressure them to conform. Bullies depend on approval and acceptance as much as chameleons, but bullies push others to agree with them instead of with others. Disagreement threatens a bully as much as it

threatens a chameleon. An extreme rebel is a poorly differentiated person too, but she pretends to be a "self" by routinely opposing the positions of others.[7]

Leaders with poor self-differentiation destroy the organizations they lead. They either become timid, making it hard for people to follow them, or they become aggressive while their employees or congregations become anxious. Poorly differentiated leaders often develop systems around them to prop up their egos. Without healthy accountability they may become narcissistic leaders of an abusive system. If they truly care about others, their lack of differentiation will turn inward, and they will abuse themselves—a common component I see among burned-out leaders. You might be thinking, "None of this describes me." Often poorly differentiated leaders are the last to know what effects they have on people because they are unsafe leaders.

Developing Differentiation of Self

The following is a list of practices for self-differentiation that helped me the most. You may not find everything on this list helpful. That's okay. Use what is useful to you. Likewise, you may discover things not on this list that are effective. Great! Go with that. Several of these steps are essential, such as spiritual practices, values, priorities, boundaries, and limits, but they all have immense value in helping you become a healthy person. Some can be done independently; others will require the help of a church, a coach, or a licensed counselor. Over the next few chapters I will explain these twelve steps you can take to become a healthy, separate person:

1. Practice mindfulness.
2. Develop spiritual practices.
3. Clarify values.
4. Identify priorities.

5. Establish boundaries.
6. Honor your limits.
7. Break destructive habits.
8. Recognize generational patterns.
9. Uncover childhood vows.
10. Silence the amplified voices.
11. Learn to remain present in conflict.
12. Respond to critics with grace.

Don't try to adopt all twelve steps at once; that would be over-whelming. Take it slow and be patient with God and with yourself. God often works slower than we would like. Trust in the slow work of God. He knows what he's doing. I incorporated these practices into my life bit by bit, sometimes starting with just a portion of a step but continually moving forward.

I needed help in doing this work, and I believe you will too. In conversation, another person can reflect what you are saying and how they see you changing. You may want to ask a few trusted people, "How do you experience me?" Give them the freedom to be honest with you, and listen to their responses without becoming defensive or judgmental. Just receive their experience of you as valid from their perspective. After you have done some differentiation work, you can ask the question again or ask, "How have you seen me change?" An outside view from several people will help you discover patterns in how you show up in the room. Just be careful that your sense of self doesn't depend on their responses; remain rooted in the love of God and your unity with Christ.

PRACTICE MINDFULNESS

To become healthy, separate selves, we must become aware of what's happening in us and around us. Mindfulness helps us develop this awareness. Many Christians are skeptical of mindfulness because they only know how it is practiced in Eastern religions or in secular psychology. Christian mindfulness has a different purpose. Charles Stone, author of *Holy Noticing: The Bible, Your Brain, and the Mindful Space Between Moments*, says, "Holy noticing is an ancient Christian practice that helps us flourish spiritually and engage the present moment to pause and notice what is happening *now*, all with a holy purpose."[8] *Holy noticing* is the phrase Stone uses for Christian mindfulness. "Holy noticing is a way to bring intentional awareness in the present moment to what and who is around us and what we're doing, thinking, and feeling—all from God's perspective."[9] These descriptions of Christian mindfulness are helpful, and from here on *mindfulness* will refer to this kind of holy noticing.

When we practice mindfulness, we are paying attention to three things. First, we experience God's presence with us. Second, we notice what is happening around us—the actions and reactions of our environment and the people who occupy it. Third, we are aware of our own thoughts, feelings, attitudes, and actions.

Psalm 139 is a summary of mindfulness. David is not only aware that God is present but also that there is nothing beyond God's awareness, not even David's inner thoughts. David is also aware of the evil things that people are doing around him. At the end of the psalm, David asks for God's perspective on the whole situation:

> Search me, God, and know my heart;
>   test me and know my anxious thoughts.
> See if there is any offensive way in me,
>   and lead me in the way everlasting. (vv. 23–24)

This is the essence of mindfulness: to gain God's perspective on what is happening in and around us.

To become more aware of my environment, I like to sit quietly and just listen. At first this is hard, but as you practice listening, it becomes more natural. And soon you will be able to enter awareness in almost any moment.

To become mindful, find a comfortable spot where you can sit with good posture. Close your eyes and listen to your environment. Don't just listen for what is loud or obvious. Listen for the quiet, close sounds and the soft, faraway sounds. Start this practice at home in a quiet room. Notice everything. As your skill grows, move to a quiet space outdoors, such as a park, woods, or field. Finally, move into a more crowded space, such as a classroom, church, or mall. When you become good at noticing the sounds around you, you'll be able to pick out the smallest noises in a crowded and busy space.

Now do the same thing with each of your senses. What do you see, smell, taste? How do things feel in your hands and on your body? For example, sitting in the park you may hear a squirrel in the trees, see the light filtering through the leaves, smell the earthiness of the grass, taste the freshness of the air, and feel the cool moisture of the ground. What are the people around you doing? Can you imagine how they might feel by what you can see and hear?

I love to go people watching at stores. I rarely do it as a discipline; it usually happens while I am waiting for my wife. I unobtrusively observe others without making them feel uncomfortable. I use my senses to gather information. Then, using my imagination, I try to empathize with them, to feel what they may be feeling in the moment.

Each observed interaction is unique. For example, I watched a mother whose little child was crying as they walked past. The mother looked frustrated and tired. "Why is this child crying?" I thought to myself. Shortly after they walked past, I got a whiff of that unmistakable odor that every parent knows. My suspicions were confirmed as they walked into the family bathroom. That child needed a new diaper and possibly a change of clothes. As a parent, I was able to empathize for what that mom was experiencing. Changing a child's diaper is never a pleasant experience, and the need arises at the most inconvenient times. I felt a twinge of her frustration as I walked away. In that moment I was mindful of myself, my surroundings, and my neighbor.

Moments like these help us develop awareness of what others may be feeling as we talk with them. Develop curiosity in each moment. Why is this person saying this? What is their body language telling me? How might their background story contribute to how they are acting? Some of these things can be observed, but you will need to ask questions to know the full story.

You should also notice how the emotions of the people in your environment are affecting you. Is there an angry customer yelling in your face? How does that make you feel? Do you find yourself becoming angry and defensive? Your anger is the fruit of what's happening internally, but what's the root cause? What inside you is leading you to feel this way? If you aren't aware of what is happening internally, you may be tempted to blame others for your behavior. Most burned-out leaders blame others for things that they should take responsibility for.

Learn to be aware of what you are feeling in the moment. Name your feelings and notice where they come from in you. Peel back the layers until you discover the root of the emotion. If I were to ask, "Why are you feeling this way?" you should be able to tell the whole story from root to fruit. "I'm angry because that customer is yelling at me, but what is really going on is . . ." Mindfulness means developing awareness of how our deep motivations, wounds, and fears are affecting us in the moment.

Often these stories go all the way back to our childhood and the defense mechanisms we created to protect ourselves. When I was working at a bookstore, I once had a customer yell at me, and I suddenly became aware that I was thinking of my father. The anger I felt came from a time my father yelled at me for something that wasn't my fault. I projected that anger back onto this customer. Perhaps they were doing something similar to me. This awareness allowed me to take a breath and respond to the customer with compassion and curiosity.

What are your emotional triggers? What makes you angry, sad, happy? What are your typical responses to each trigger? Do your emotions take over, or are you able to notice them and insert a pause before responding? What are some healthy ways you could respond in each situation? These questions will help you develop a plan that will enable you to notice and respond to your emotional triggers in mindful ways.

Mindfulness isn't just for introverts. In fact, extroverts sometimes find greater benefit from the practice because it doesn't come naturally for them. It stretches them to become more fully developed human beings. (Conversely, introverts often need to practice community with others to stretch themselves.) As you practice mindfulness, you will better notice what others are feeling and how their feelings affect you. You will begin to notice what is happening inside you and be able to release these thoughts and emotions so that you can be fully present to others.

A MINDFULNESS PRACTICE

Here's a short mindfulness practice you can do right now.[10] This should take about ten minutes to complete. As you become more skilled at it, you may choose to expand the time. Find a comfortable place where you can sit with good posture and follow the steps below.

1. Start by focusing your attention on God's presence with you in this moment. During this whole practice, if you find your mind wandering, return to awareness of God's presence.
2. Breathe slowly and deeply in through your nose and out through your mouth. If it helps you focus, count to four as you breathe in, hold your breath for four beats, exhale to the count of four, and hold for four before starting the pattern

over. As you breathe deeply don't raise your chest or shoulders; let your breath fill your lungs and push down into your belly. How does each breath make you feel? What do you feel as you breathe in? What happens in your body as you breathe out? How is this breathing affecting your emotions?

3. Starting at the top of your head and working your way through each muscle group down to your feet, notice any aches, pains, tension, or numbness. Are you able to focus on that muscle and relax it until the feeling goes away? Try tensing the muscle, hold it for a few seconds, and as you release, notice how it feels the moment the muscle relaxes. Try to replicate that feeling as you relax each muscle group. Think of releasing the tension through your feet into the ground. Some people find it helpful to stand barefoot in the grass.

4. Continue to breathe deeply and relax. Now take a few moments to listen to your environment as described earlier in the chapter. Listen deeply for the soft, quiet, and faraway sounds as well as the louder noises. What can you notice with your other senses—sight, smell, taste, touch?

5. Turn your noticing inward. What are you feeling? Without judging, notice and name each feeling and release it to God in prayer.

6. Notice your thoughts. What are you thinking about? Think about your thinking. Notice not just what you are thinking but how you are thinking about it. Are you being critical, judgmental, worried, anxious? Again, notice without judging and release these thoughts to God. If you need to, jot the thoughts on a piece of paper to get them out of your head.

7. Now spend some time in prayer noticing God's love: his presence with you, his goodness toward you, and his protection over you. Receive this love from God and offer your own love back to him. Quiet your soul in silence with God as a child with a loving parent. What is God saying to you in this

moment? Silently offer yourself up to God. What does your soul want to say to God? Tell him.

8. Sit in silence a few more moments then stand and stretch. Take this focus with you into the rest of your day or use it to enter into your Bible reading.

Regular use of this practice will help you become more aware in every area of your life. It will reduce your anxiety in the moment and help you pause to make healthier choices. When I'm healthy, I practice this for thirty to sixty minutes a few times per week. If I find myself becoming too reactive, I return to daily practice of mindfulness for a while.

In the next chapter, we will explore some spiritual practices that can help us differentiate from others as we commune with God. Here are some questions to help you reflect on this chapter:

1. Are you an overly responsible person? List some ways that you try to control what others can and should do for themselves?

2. In what ways are you looking for approval or validation from others?

3. How have you seen your own insecurity show up? Do you fall into people pleasing? Do you bully others into compliance?

4. Are you able to distinguish your own values, priorities, and boundaries from the people around you? How do you know?

5. When others are anxious, angry, or fearful, how do you respond? Do their emotions infect you, or are you able to let them experience their emotions while remaining calm, attentive, and present?

10

SOUL CARE

One of the most shocking discoveries of my burnout was realizing that my soul had become as dry as a desert. I was trying to pour life-giving water into others, but my reservoir was empty. I believe the most important step toward becoming separate and healthy is to *develop regular spiritual practices* that deepen your relationship with God and reinforce your identity in Christ. There are some practices—Bible reading, prayer, corporate worship, and Sabbath keeping—that every Christian leader should follow because they are essential to our spiritual health. Some of these may be different than what you've come to expect, so pay attention. If our old ways aren't working, maybe a new approach will help. In learning to care for our souls we are following the pattern of Jesus. Through these practices we learn what Jesus meant when he said, "Whoever drinks the water I give them will never thirst. Indeed, the water I give them will become in them a spring of water welling up to eternal life" (John 4:14).

BIBLE READING

Every Christian needs a connection to the Word of God. For some of us this means reading short selections of Scripture daily. Others find it helpful to read large portions, even whole books of the Bible in one sitting. Some prefer slow, thoughtful reading. Others find it helpful to listen to the Word being read using their favorite Bible app. Your approach to Scripture should be based on what works best for you. Your personality, learning style, and the amount of time you set aside will determine your approach. Find a mix of both broad and narrow readings of Scripture. Read whole books, but also spend time in smaller stories, single paragraphs, or even just one verse. Your time in the Word will help center you in God's love for you and give you a more grounded sense of reality.

We need to learn to read the Bible in three dimensions. First, we should be reading for understanding. This involves reading the text, studying it in its context, and engaging in good interpretive practices. This is essential for rightly understanding God and self. Reading for understanding provides guardrails that keep us from error. Most pastors and Bible teachers use this first kind of reading to prepare lessons or sermons. However, if the other two types of reading are missing, their lessons and sermons will lack wisdom and depth. The same is true for you: if you only read for understanding, you will likely become puffed up or one dimensional.

Second, we should read to nourish our own souls. This is reading for refreshment and relating to God in the text. It is more about communing with the Holy Spirit through the Word and less about studying the text. In this type of reading, we are aware of God's presence with us, and we are allowing him to lead us into his story. Reading should engage our imagination and awaken our senses as we allow ourselves to connect emotionally with Scripture. This intimate, one-on-one time with God happens as we sit at Jesus's feet and listen to the Holy Spirit.

Reading for refreshment is just for you, a time when you experience the love God has for you in Christ. It's not reading to get a sermon or lesson. In fact, it may be helpful to practice the discipline of secrecy with this reading. Secrecy is keeping to yourself what the Holy Spirit has shown you until it has a chance to settle in your soul and become part of you. We wait until there is clear direction from the Holy Spirit before we offer it to others. The practice of *Lectio Divina* can be helpful in nourishing our souls in Christ.

Lectio Divina ("divine reading") is a way of reading Scripture deeply, slowly, and contemplatively. As we read, we are focusing on God's presence and listening attentively to the Holy Spirit. It's more about experiencing relationship with God through the text than interpreting it. There are typically four movements to lectio (reading, meditation, prayer, and contemplation).

The third dimension of Scripture reading is meditation, the deliberate internalizing of Scripture for heart transformation. Instead of looking for ways the Bible can prove our presuppositions and biases, *we allow the Word to read us and change us.* This is what it means to hide God's Word in our hearts (Ps. 119:11). We spend time opening our inner life to the love of God until his love becomes our love. We are being changed by the Scriptures at the core of our being so that our behavior naturally flows from a heart that loves God, self, and others. We are learning to live from the new heart the Holy Spirit has given us and cooperating with the Spirit's work to conform us into the image of Jesus.

All three dimensions of Bible reading are necessary for Christian leaders. If we focus only on reading for understanding, our leadership, teaching, or preaching will be cold and academic. If we ignore reading for understanding, our response to Scripture will be purely subjective and lack truth, and we will lead people astray. Failing to nourish our souls in Scripture will lead to burnout because God will seem distant and demanding. Neglecting meditation leaves us stuck and frustrated because change comes slowly when we resist the work of the Holy Spirit. You must determine the rhythms and seasons that you need for each dimension of Scripture reading.

Pastors are particularly tempted to read Scripture only to get their next sermon. I get it—that's where vocational pressure and the tyranny of the urgent push us. We have to resist this urge. All our Scripture reading should help us relate to God. Reading Scripture isn't just a task to accomplish; it's a relationship to explore. The refreshment and nourishment we get for our souls and the heart change that comes from meditation are tangible ways that God expresses his loving relationship with us as our Father. Reducing pastoral ministry to a job is not healthy. If we are following Jesus, we will recognize that everything he did and said came from relationship with the Father.

PRAYER

Prayer is essential to developing a healthy separation of self. Unfortunately, most Christians approach prayer as simply asking God for things. We ask God to feed our desires, fix our relationships, or remove our discomforts instead of asking God what *he* wants for us. In the Lord's Prayer, Jesus taught his disciples that prayer is about seeking God and his will in worship before we ask for our own needs. We acknowledge God's name as special and submit to his will; these are the primary movements of prayer. As we spend time with the Father, seeking his face, receiving his love, learning his will, and shaping our own wills to match his, our requests change. By the time we get to "give us this day our daily bread," our whole perspective on what we need and want has changed. When we seek God and his will first, then we can ask *according to his will.* This transforms prayer completely.

Part of my recovery from burnout was learning to spend more of my prayer time becoming aware of God's presence and submitting to his will. I used mindfulness, silence, and solitude as spiritual disciplines to help me notice God and his love presently with me. As a result, my prayers became more focused. My frustration with God diminished as my contentment in him increased. I became more stable emotionally and more at ease with myself and others. I felt less anxious because I was no longer taking responsibility for things that belong to God. I was able to relax into God's will and receive each day and each encounter as a gift. By learning to pray from an awareness of God's presence and in submission to his will, I was able to live and lead with much more confidence. My reality was now rooted in God's plan not mine.

When our times in prayer become a duty or obligation, prayer itself can become a chore. When I find myself approaching prayer in that way, I meditate on Psalm 131:1–2:

> O LORD, my heart is not lifted up;
>> my eyes are not raised too high;
> I do not occupy myself with things
>> too great and too marvelous for me.
> But I have calmed and quieted my soul,
>> like a weaned child with its mother;
>> like a weaned child is my soul within me. (ESV)

This psalm helps me come to God as a little child. I imagine my soul being comforted by God in the same way children find comfort with their mother. I no longer approach God as a tired, dutiful servant but as a beloved child. Sometimes, as I sit in silence, it's as if I can feel the Father's loving embrace. This is prayer: enjoying intimacy with God and seeking God's will before asking for God's provision.

When we prayerfully fill our souls with God's love and care instead of emptying our wants and desires onto God, we become more resilient and assertive. By seeking God's will in our hearts and for our communities before we ask for God's provision, we have more confidence for each day. We no longer have to generate confidence from within because we are following God's lead, not our own ideas. When our hearts are shaped by God's will first, asking for the desires of our hearts becomes asking God for the provision and power to accomplish his will. These are the things God delights to provide.

This doesn't mean prayer is never like wrestling with God or that we stop coming to him with requests. However, we no longer blame God for not giving what we ask. Instead, we realize that (1) we are not fully submitting to God's will and are asking for the wrong things or (2) we are waiting on God's timing. In both situations, we can experience God's love for us, and he doesn't have to feel distant anymore. When we pray for God's will—nothing more, nothing less, and nothing else—*everything* becomes a gift from God. Even in our darkest moments, we know that God's will and God's love are at work in our lives.

CORPORATE WORSHIP

Corporate worship is important because we are blessed by the real, physical presence of other believers. Singing together, hugging each other, and sharing meals are part of this blessing. Conversations are easier when we can read the body language of other people. There is something about watching others as we worship God that builds our faith.

Years ago we joined my brother's family at their church—a large, multicultural church in Washington, DC. It was refreshing to worship outside the isolated, white culture of the small church where I served in rural northern Michigan. Just before the worship service began, a tall, muscular Black man sat down directly in front of me. He unashamedly wept with joy as he sang of God's love. This man's love for God inspired and expanded my faith in ways that continue years later. After the service, I approached him and said, "I was sitting right behind you this morning. Your worship was beautiful to me.

Thank you." He smiled broadly as tears welled up in his eyes. And he said, "You have no idea how much that means to me." We never learned each other's names, but our faith was made stronger that day.

We gather with other people to worship God, to celebrate his love, and to be reminded of his grace. We hear the stories and teachings of Jesus and are together led by the Holy Spirit. We remind one another of the grounding reality of our lives: we are fully and permanently loved by God in Jesus Christ. The presence of other people exalting God above all makes this reality tangible.

As part of your recovery from burnout, find a place where you can worship God with other people. Look for safe, mature Christians in the church and ask them to walk with you through confession, absolution, repentance, and restoration. They may be elders in your church, a small group, or just one or two trusted friends. Be a safe person for them too. Try to be the people who embody this beautiful word from 2 Corinthians 1:3–5:

> Praise be to the God and Father of our Lord Jesus Christ, the Father of compassion and the God of all comfort, who comforts us in all our troubles, so that we can comfort those in any trouble with the comfort we ourselves receive from God. For just as we share abundantly in the sufferings of Christ, so also our comfort abounds through Christ.

Corporate worship should be the physical manifestation of God's love and grace through the church to the world. We need to be reminded of God's love in these tangible ways.

Pastors, you need to be in corporate worship too—not always on the stage but among the congregation from time to time. You can be so preoccupied with facilitating worship that you miss some of the critical elements of worship that your soul needs. I encourage pastors to spend at least one Sunday each month out of the pulpit and off the stage. That may mean bringing in special speakers, training up other preachers, or sharing more of the preaching load with other pastors on staff. Pastors who burn out usually need extended time away from the church before they can enter worship in a healthy way again. By taking time to worship in your own congregation or in other churches, you will be receiving the blessing that can prevent this extreme measure from becoming necessary.

SABBATH

The most important spiritual practice in my recovery from burnout was Sabbath. The word *Sabbath* literally means "to cease or stop." If Christian leaders have trouble doing one thing, it's stopping. We are so driven to produce, accomplish, and grow that we forget God's command to cease. I'm astonished how ignoring this commandment often garners praise among Christians. We don't observe the commandment out of duty to the law but as a gift from God for our good. Pastors and Christian ministry leaders who ignore the Sabbath are choosing an unhealthy path and should be corrected. Instead, they are usually given raises and bigger platforms. No wonder Christian leaders are burning out at such an alarming rate.

Jesus reminds us that God commanded the Sabbath for our good (Mark 2:27), and his commands are a blessing. With the Sabbath, God is giving us what we need for health and resilience. In the first appendix, I provide a simple guide for planning your Sabbath.[1] As you plan, I encourage you to incorporate the following three elements: cease, receive, and enjoy.

Cease

The Sabbath starts by *ceasing from our work* for a period of twenty-four hours. Traditionally, the Jewish Sabbath started at sundown on Friday and continued to sundown on Saturday. I commend the practice of starting your Sabbath at sundown. Begin with a nice but simple meal with family or friends. In the Christian church, the Saturday Sabbath was eventually replaced by the Lord's Day (i.e., Sunday). However, this doesn't mean that they eliminated the practices of the Sabbath. The early church continued to meet weekly, and many considered Sunday to be their day of rest. I'm not sure how Sunday became a day of busyness and productivity instead of rest, but it's time we returned to the practice of making a Sabbath day a priority.

Alongside weekly Sabbaths, the Hebrew people observed seven holy feast days (also called Sabbaths) in the Old Testament Jewish calendar. On these days the people did no work for that twenty-four-hour period (see Lev. 23).

Planning a Sabbath starts by setting aside one twenty-four-hour period each week. On this day we will do no work—ceasing productivity, planning, accomplishment, or earning.[2] Instead of the active work of making and doing, we focus on passively receiving God's love and provision. If a full twenty-four hours seems like too much, start by finding chunks of time throughout the week that add up to twenty-four. Soon you will find that these islands of refreshment are not enough to satisfy your soul, and soon you will prioritize planning one full day.

Receive and Enjoy

On the Sabbath we *receive and enjoy God and his goodness* through the gifts that he offers. We spend special, leisurely time with God in his Word and prayer. We can see God's goodness better when we rest. Jesus took naps, so we can too. We are blessed by relaxed eating and fellowship around the table. We spend time with people who feed our souls and remind us of God's love. We even engage in activities we enjoy simply for the pleasure that activity brings. In other words, we have fun—something many burned-out leaders have lost. On the Sabbath we take time for wonder by listening to beautiful music, noticing God's creation, and tasting the goodness of God; all our senses are awakened to him.

The practice of regular Sabbath rest serves as a reminder that God is in control and we are not. We learn that we can step away for a full twenty-four hours and our organization (or our work) doesn't fall apart. I found that I was less stressed, more productive, and more creative after establishing a good rhythm of weekly Sabbaths. Freedom from the desire to control and from the stress of expectations allows us to relax into God's goodness and direction in our lives. As we are set free from this anxiety, we become better leaders—a nonanxious presence for our church or team. Taking time to enjoy God and his goodness, to have worship-filled fun, and to be with people who replenish our souls will counteract the effects of burnout.

The Sabbath can also be a time to lament, a chance to bring all our negative emotions to God. Anger, grief, sadness, and frustration are all welcomed by God when we are honest with him in faith. By finding healthy ways to express these unwanted emotions in God's presence, we open ourselves to experience positive emotions like happiness, joy, hope, and peace. All but one of the psalms of lament end with an expression of faith or hope in God. As the psalmists express their anger or grief, they are freed to see the goodness of God again. Lament is an essential part of burnout recovery and helps us develop healthy emotional separation from others. For a short guide on how to plan your own Sabbath and a list of resources to help with this, see appendix 1, "Planning Your Sabbath."

OTHER DISCIPLINES

Many other spiritual disciplines can be useful for differentiation of self. I encourage you to playfully explore what works for you. By "playfully" I mean that you don't have to do it perfectly; relax into the enjoyment and benefits each discipline offers. If it starts to feel routine, move on to another practice. The next chapter explores the practices of clarifying your values, priorities, and boundaries. This requires time for reflection. Healthy Sabbath practice will be a boon to working through burnout and building resilience. Here are some questions to help you reflect on your own soul care:

1. Describe the last time you enjoyed the act of reading Scripture as a way to relate with God.
2. What are some Scripture passages that you have memorized? Rehearse them now and ask yourself, "How have these passages worked their way into my soul?"
3. Evaluate your life of prayer. Does it feel like a real relationship, or do you feel like you are talking to the air? What needs to change so that you are both listening to and talking with God?
4. What are three to five beginning steps that will help you develop a healthy Sabbath practice?
5. What would it look like to make your Sabbath day the best, most physically and spiritually refreshing day of the week?

11

BOUNDARIES

Peppermint Princess Lee, my childhood pet, was a large German Shepherd. She came to our family when the Lee family moved to China. We shortened her name to Pepper. She was a beautiful dog with lots of energy, and we enjoyed watching her chase rabbits and squirrels around the backyard. Squirrels would run up a tree and jump onto the garage where Pepper couldn't see them. Rabbits, however, had a more difficult time. They tried to escape under our three-foot white picket fence, but the barrier was no match for a young German Shepherd. Pepper vaulted the fence with ease and chased the rabbit down the grass-covered alley behind our house. She would end up lost, tired, and alone. Occasionally, a neighbor called us, but we usually had to go looking for her. We'd find her panting in someone else's yard or relaxing on their front porch. Thankfully, no one called animal control to have Pepper removed from their property. After a while, my dad got sick of chasing the dog all over our suburban Chicago neighborhood. So he built a six-foot privacy fence. She only tried to jump that fence once. After that, whenever a rabbit dug its way under our fence, Pepper positioned herself between the rabbit and the hole. Not many rabbits survived that encounter.

Many leaders are like Pepper. They chase after their vision and leap over boundaries in the process. Soon they find themselves lost and in trouble. In crossing these boundaries, they unintentionally hurt their families, friends, and coworkers. In their lust to "catch the rabbit," they run themselves down. Tired and stuck, they search for another rabbit to chase. Bouncing from one vision to another is a sign of an immature leader who doesn't know who they are or where their boundaries lie. In this chapter, we will explore the motivations behind what we do as leaders and how to clarify what we really want so we don't go chasing rabbits.

CLARIFY VALUES

Whenever I'm coaching a leader through burnout, early in the process we discuss values. Your core values are the beliefs and ideals that drive your behavior. We are always driven by our values, but most burned-out leaders aren't aware of the values driving them. They act out of hidden beliefs that lead to negative results, and when they actually look at what's behind their behavior, they discover unhealthy or destructive values. Because of our sinfulness, shame, and brokenness, we all have default beliefs like this.

Living in a way that goes against your true core values is called *moral injury.* You hurt yourself when you act against your basic morality. One of the signs you are suffering from moral injury is displaced anger—a feeling of sudden anger, even rage, that seems to come from nowhere. One of the keys to working your way out of burnout is to clarify what you value. This will give you the tools to see how you have been operating against your values and how you can choose a different path. Instead of operating on autopilot, you can choose new, healthy values that will help you be your true self.

How then does one discover and choose these core values? It can't be done in a few hours. You need time for regular, personal reflection and analysis (and even some negotiating with yourself). I recommend to my clients that they spend at least thirty to sixty minutes a day until what they truly value becomes crystal clear. Below are some steps to discovering your core values. Be sure you've first begun the work from earlier chapters of becoming whole and secure, otherwise you may end up with values that work against your identity in Christ.

Learn What Values Are

The first step in clarifying your values is to understand what a value is. Values are the moral code that guides what we do. They are the root beliefs that tell us who we are and what we need to do to be healthy and successful. Our values energize us and tell us who we want to be.

My coaching clients sometimes struggle to understand what is and is not a value. For example, they might start by saying, "I value relationships." That's vague. Which relationships? What kinds or qualities of relationships do you value? Why do you value relationships? You will know when you have defined a core value when it is *personal*, *foundational*, and *motivating*.

A core value is *personal* in that it must come from the heart, the core of who you are. It must be *your* value, or it will have no power in your life. Your values are unique to you because they express who you are and who you want to become. Values express your identity.

A core value is *foundational*. It must be simple and clear, not vague. It's the bedrock. If you can dig down and find a deeper motivation, you haven't found a core value. I tell my clients to keep digging until they can't go deeper. Sometimes it helps to have a friend, coach, counselor, or spiritual director ask you some hard questions to see if you are really at your foundational beliefs.

Finally, a core value is a *motivational* force in your life. It isn't an intellectually detached idea that makes no difference in how you live. Core beliefs energize you and inspire action. Your core beliefs demand movement in a certain direction. James 2:20 says, "Faith without deeds is useless." In the same way, if our beliefs don't move us forward, they aren't core values.

Ask Yourself Hard Questions

Now you can begin to ask yourself the hard questions: What motivates you? What drives you? What lights you up? What sucks the life out of you? What should the world be like? What do you believe about God, self, and humanity? What are you willing to die for? Who are the most important people in your life? Why do you do what you do? What does the best version of you look like? Who do you want to become and why?

These questions should be penetrating and take thought and effort to answer like the ones above. Stay away from questions about your job description or other temporary things. If you can't develop them on your own, find someone who can help you drill down into your heart to unearth your deepest motivations.[1]

Make a List of Who and What You Value

Now write out a list of your values. Your list might have twenty words or phrases, or it might have two hundred. Just be sure you get it all down on paper. Write it by hand. Whether it's because we see something in our own hand or because it takes longer to write, writing by hand ignites our creativity and helps us connect with our true selves.

Take time to reflect on your values before finalizing your list. Go back over the answers to your questions. Whittle down the picture of who you want to be to its essential elements. Eliminate redundancy and work toward a clear picture of your true self. Now narrow down the list to your twenty most important values. Choose the ones that hold the most power for you. Maybe they are the most inspiring or most needed or most energizing. They should be the twenty words or phrases that give you the clearest picture of your best self.

Define Your Values

Taking your list of twenty core values, write out your own definition for each one. What does this word or phrase mean? Work on the definitions until they are clear. Craft the wording of each definition until you are sure that each word is precisely the right word in exactly the right place. Once you have your definitions clear, pick your top ten and prioritize them. What is the single most important value in your life? What is the next most important? Write out your top ten values and definitions in order. (Don't discard the other ten, but don't worry about prioritizing them.)

Compare Your List to Your Life

Now look at your list of priorities and ask yourself, "Does this list inform how I am living right now?" You may discover that your list of core values doesn't match your life. In this process, most of my clients find it helpful to make a list of the values their life currently expresses and compare it to the list of their actual core values. This can be a revealing exercise. Many find that they are living opposite of their core values. Resist the natural urge to become disgusted or angry with yourself. You are finally seeing yourself clearly, perhaps for the first time. That's a good thing! Now you have a way to move forward.

Once you have made your values crystal clear, you are ready to reshape your life with hope for a better future you. You will want to know your core values by heart or carry them with you wherever you go. They will form the basis for the next few steps of becoming a healthy, separate self. The first step is using your core values to identify your priorities in life.

ESTABLISH PRIORITY

Let's think about what it means to prioritize. The word *priority* means the one thing that comes before all others, so you can really have only one priority. We tend to think that we can have multiple priorities. After all, don't we talk about our priorities in life? Greg McKeown, author of *Essentialism*, straightens us out:

> The word *priority* came into the English language in the 1400s. It was singular. It meant the very first or prior thing. It stayed singular for the next five hundred years. Only in the 1900s did we pluralize the term and start talking about *priorities*. Illogically, we reasoned that by changing the word we could bend reality. Somehow we would now be able to have multiple "first" things. People and companies routinely try to do just that. . . .
>
> But when we try to do it all and have it all, we find ourselves making trade-offs at the margins that we would never take on as our intentional strategy. When we don't purposefully and deliberately choose where to focus our energies and time, other people—our bosses, our colleagues, our clients, and even our families—will choose for us, and before long we'll have lost sight of everything that is meaningful and important.[7]

When we try to have multiple priorities, they compete with one another, and we end up having no priority at all. It's like having a compass that doesn't point north. As a leader you will need to have clarity on which of your relationships, tasks, and dreams is most important. This is where your work on values will be of great help. You have already determined what drives you as a person. Now you can apply those values to prioritize your life.

You may be tempted to divide your priorities into categories—personal priorities, family priorities, work priorities, and religious priorities. This type of compartmentalization will just divide your life and make one area compete with another. If you find yourself trying to balance these areas, then you aren't approaching life as a whole person. This division will eventually lead you right back into burnout.

We can really have only one priority, one thing that is most important in your life. Figuring this out is *the* key to living with integrity. Your one thing that comes before all other things is what you will worship. Everything else in your life must bow to this one thing. Jesus highlighted this when talking with the rich young ruler (Luke 18:22) and with Martha (Luke 10:42). Jesus called each of them to leave everything they thought was important and put their relationship with him first. Being a Christian means that following Jesus is our priority, our *one thing* that comes before all others. He must be our highest value and greatest love.

What is the one thing in your life that comes before all else? If you are wise, it will be a relationship. If you are a Christian, it will be your relationship with God through Jesus. But you must make this decision for yourself. You can only pick one. What's it going to be? What is the single most important thing in your life, the one thing that *must* come before all others? Take your time. This is important.

Don't move on until you've found your one thing. You may find yourself wrestling with competing loves. That's good so long as only one love is standing in the end. There are no shortcuts here. All attempts to get around this reality will divide us and lead us back to self-destructive behavior and burnout. Having more than one greatest love is infidelity. You are being unfaithful to yourself, to your greatest love, and to all lesser loves.

This process will take time—maybe months or even years. You will probably experience feelings of grief and loss as things you love deeply are forced to take a back seat to what you love most. You may experience shame as you confess you have tried to love multiple things at the same time. It's rare to find someone who has followed through on this work. They have the uncompromising force of conviction. If you want to overcome your people pleasing, your perfectionism, or your shame, this is key: *you can have only one love.*

At this point you may want to push back: "But I love God, my spouse, my kids, and my church. How can I choose just one?" I'm not saying you must stop loving your spouse or your kids. In fact, you can't truly love any of them until you figure out which one comes first. Finding your first love will help you put all other loves in order. The first one is the most difficult to discern because it means choosing which other loves cannot be first.

As part of my recovery from burnout, I decided that my love for God, in and through Jesus, must come first. This wasn't the first time I had made that decision. In fact, most of my life has been a series of decisions about who I would love first. However, this time I began to see that by loving God first, his love can flow through me to all my other loves. The choice wasn't really between God and my wife or God and my son. It was between God and me. All my other loves were really an expression of my love of self. It wasn't until I surrendered to God that I was able to truly, unselfishly love myself and others.

If you have the courage to discover it, your first love—your one thing, your priority—will help you put everything in order. Listen to your values. What do they say you love the most? Do you need to reevaluate them? This period of your recovery may feel like a series of negotiations, and that's okay, so long as you find the clarity of having one priority.

After you have discovered your one thing, your greatest love, you can begin to establish what is secondary. Again, don't break up your life into compartments. What is the second most important thing in your whole life? Be sure that this second thing remains under your first love. For me, the second most important thing in my life is my own soul. If I am to truly express my love for others, I need to learn to love myself as God loves me. My first love is teaching me how to live. I decided that my soul had to come second because if I am not healthy, whole, and separate from others, I can't really love them as they deserve. My brokenness will end up hurting all my other relationships.

Once you have set your priority, you can determine what comes next. Don't allow your values to compete at any level. Your second value comes after your priority but before everything else. Discern this and then move on to number three. Keep working through the process until you have your top ten relationships, behaviors, or things that are most important in your life. There can be no ties, and your priorities cannot be fluid, moving up or down the list based on circumstances. If that happens, it means you aren't yet clear on which is most important. There may be times when you choose to go against this priority ranking, but those choices should be rare and based on your true core values.

Failure to be clear and strict on your priority is one of the main reasons leaders burn out. They find themselves trying to do too many things at once. For example, have you ever tried to please both work and family at the same time. When I try this, my family feels neglected and my work suffers. It's better to be crystal clear on which is more important. For me, I always want to be sure my family is well cared for and experiences my love before dedicating time to my work. This way when I have to take time for urgent work matters, or travel for a few days, my family doesn't feel neglected. They know they come first because I've demonstrated it over and over. One of the hardest lessons from my burnout was learning that my family felt neglected because of my ministry. I don't want them to ever feel that again.

As you establish your top ten, be sure you have reasons why they must fall in this order. Write out your reasons in case you are tempted to get things out of order. Clarity is key. Just as you worked for clarity in your values, so too you must be clear on your priority and your reasons for making these choices.

The question I most often ask myself is "What is most important right now?" To answer that question, I must know my values and my priority. This also helps me establish boundaries that will keep me healthy, whole, and separate.

ESTABLISH BOUNDARIES

Boundaries are rules you put in place for yourself to ensure that you are not violating, diminishing, or harming the personhood of others and that they aren't violating yours. Like a fence between neighbors, boundaries work both ways. Henry Cloud, author of *Boundaries* and *Boundaries for Leaders*, says, "Boundaries define us. They define *what is me* and *what is not me*. A boundary shows me where I end and someone else begins, leading to a sense of ownership."[3] We all need boundaries to ensure that we are remaining a whole, healthy, and separate self.

Boundaries keep us from taking ownership of what is not ours. Many burned-out leaders have been overresponsible in their life and leadership. Taking responsibility for things that are beyond their control, they borrow worries and concerns that are not theirs to carry. Additionally, the people who *are* responsible are robbed of their opportunity to grow and act as mature adults. Leaders who lack boundaries may try to control the emotions of others by withholding information or manipulating the situation. Their good intentions cause them to be manipulating and controlling because they are not letting others carry their own responsibilities. Healthy boundaries allow the leader to maintain ownership and control over their emotions, actions, and responsibilities. They allow the leader to say no with conviction, and they prevent the leader from saying yes to the wrong things.

We all have individuals in our lives who lack boundaries and don't respect us as people. Good boundaries help us to be assertive when others mistreat us. For example, if someone is manipulative, controlling, or critical, a healthy boundary will tell us that this person is not good for our mental health and well-being. So we establish that boundary with the manipulative person by expressing our own dignity, asserting our values, and saying no to their attempts to control.

People who don't respect our boundaries may get angry with us when we first establish boundaries with them. Or we may get angry with ourselves when we realize that we have been violating our own boundaries or letting others violate them. We cannot control the anger of others; we must let them be angry without letting their anger control our thoughts, emotions, or actions. We must not beat up ourselves for our lack of boundaries in the past. Growth means forgiving ourselves for those mistakes while ensuring that they don't happen again.

Honoring the individuality and separateness of others without disconnecting from them is essential to healthy relationships. This is hard. We may become so focused on others that we violate our own personhood by letting them overstep our boundaries. Or we may become so self-protective that we shut others out. Good boundaries help us to remain relationally connected to people. In fact, the better our boundaries, the healthier our relationships will be.

Look back over your values and your priority list. They will help you determine where you need to establish boundaries. Have you been living in a way that is opposed to your values? What boundaries do you need to establish to ensure that your values are honored? You may be tempted to violate your first love. What rules can you establish for yourself that will help you to keep your priority clear? Are there people in your life who influence you to violate your values or priority? Are they willing to change, or do they need to be removed from your life? Be sure you respect them enough to tell them your decision first.

This is how we know we have good, healthy boundaries.[4] We don't try to avoid or diminish the consequences of actions for ourselves or others. We respect others to make their own decisions. We admit we can't change on our own and we need help from God and others. We respect the boundaries of others. We experience freedom and love, not anger or fear. We are concerned with how our boundaries are affecting others and renegotiate them for the well-being of everyone involved. We are proactive, not reactive. We offer only what we already possess without envying what others have. We are active and assertive, engaging in self-leadership and self-control. We clearly communicate and continually maintain our boundaries. We remove the barriers to relational connection.

To establish and maintain healthy boundaries, they must flow out of your core values and express your prioritized life. Like the fence my father built to keep our dog from escaping the yard, boundaries that are not maintained become worthless. If you establish a boundary but fail to enforce it, people will soon be walking through the holes in your fence. Burned out leaders have broken-down boundaries.

Boundaries are not just rules we establish for ourselves. God established boundaries for us too. So we'll close this chapter with another piece of differentiation of self: receiving and honoring our God-given limits.

HONOR YOUR LIMITS

We dream of life without limits because we think that limitlessness is freedom. But limits are good. We all have limits that God placed on us so that we can be safe, healthy, and free. Actually, limits create freedom. They give us, as finite creatures, a sense of comfort and control. For example, the limit of gravity keeps us from flying off into space. Limits of strength keep us from injury. Limits of energy open us to enjoy food and sleep.

What are your God-given limits? We all have limits on our physical endurance, emotional stamina, relational capacity, and the amount of time we can work productively. We have limits in our knowledge, insight, and spiritual understanding. We have limits on what we can and can't control. Recognizing and living within these limits will prevent you from overextending yourself. Leaders like to push their limits, but when we fail to honor our limits, we get hurt or hurt others. Athletes who push the boundaries of their physical performance end up injured and may have shortened careers. Athletes who know their limits and stop short of them, stay healthy, and have longer careers. Students who honor the limits on their energy by getting enough sleep and eating healthy meals are more likely to succeed. Students who don't honor their bodies will be tired and struggle to think clearly, and their grades will suffer.

Similarly, working more than fifty hours per week diminishes a worker's productivity.[5] Wise employers limit the number of hours their employees work so that they can operate with maximum productivity. Employers who take advantage of their employees, who require longer hours, end up with disgruntled, unproductive workers and high turnover rates.

Most burned-out leaders have ignored or disregarded their relational limits with both family and church. I once heard a prominent pastor say, "If I take care of the church, God will take care of my family." Leaders who follow this path end up divorced or have broken relationships with their children. They ignore both minimum and maximum limits by being underconnected to family and overresponsible to church.

Yes, you have minimum limits. If you don't get a minimum amount of oxygen, food, water, sleep, or activity, then you will get sick or die. In the same way, your leadership has both minimum and maximum limits. Burned-out leaders often violate their limits in *both* directions. They overwork until they crash; then they underwork to try and feel better. This pattern can't be sustained, and eventually the anxiety of both extremes catches up with them.

Some minimum limits are common to all people: oxygen, food,

sleep. We all have minimum requirements to do and keep our jobs. There are minimums we must maintain in our relationship and our finances. And if I don't get a minimum of one cup of coffee in the morning, I won't function well before lunch. What minimum limits are unique to you? I have learned that I need a minimum amount of quiet time for reflection before going to bed to have a good night's sleep, but my wife doesn't. She can fall asleep quickly and sleep soundly throughout the night without preparation.

We all have maximum limits too. As I described earlier, when I was a senior in high school, I ignored my physical limits and played basketball for almost twelve hours straight, which led to a strained back and months of painkillers and physical therapy. Since then my back can't handle as much strenuous activity as it did before. The damage is permanent, and I've had to accept that limit. Some maximum limits are unique to you. You may have physical limitations that others don't, and we all have varying emotional limits from situation to situation. What are some of your unique maximum limits?

We all have limits on how many relationships we can manage. Anthropologist Robin Dunbar calculated the relational limits we can sustain.[6] These numbers can vary from person to person based on one's personality. Extroverts will likely have more friends overall, but they usually are not as close with them. Introverts, on the other hand, may have fewer friends, but their relationships often have a deeper intimacy that extroverts rarely experience. Dunbar found that the number of casual friendships any person can maintain is between 100 and 200, with 150 being the average (often called the Dunbar number). Most of us can maintain about fifty close friendships and fifteen intimate friendships. The closest group, the most intimate relationships, is limited to five. Many burned-out leaders are pushing the maximum limits of their casual friendships while ignoring the minimum limit of five people with whom they can share their most personal needs.

We all need to identify and protect our limits to be healthy, separate people. We need to know the maximum limits that we can manage and the minimum limits that we need to sustain us. Take some time to reflect on your limits in each of the following categories:

- **PHYSICAL LIMITS:** rest, exercise, energy
- **RELATIONAL LIMITS:** family, friendships, confidants, critics, encouragers
- **EMOTIONAL LIMITS:** emotional reserves, emotional output
- **WORK LIMITS:** weekly schedule, vacation time, physical energy, time for reflection and creativity
- **SPIRITUAL LIMITS:** relationship with God, worship, spiritual friends, Sabbath

For each of the categories above, what are your minimum limits? What do you need to sustain healthy life? What are your maximum limits? What is the most you can give before you start to diminish and lose health? What boundaries do you need to establish to honor these limits? How can you build margin into your life so that you don't push beyond your limits? (*Margin* is the space we create between events or tasks so that we can pause to refresh.) How do these limits help you express values, priorities, and boundaries?

HONORING YOUR BOUNDARIES

When we have healthy boundaries that are based on our core values, come from a prioritized life, and honor our God-given limits, we enjoy health and wholeness. Good boundaries help us become assertive about our needs while remaining relationally open to the needs of others. They help us live in freedom by defining where our danger zones are and what is likely to cause us harm. I once heard someone say that the power of "no" is in a stronger "yes." Boundaries based on priority help us say yes to the right things and empower us to say no so we are no longer trapped by things we should not be doing.

If you're ever going to break free from the cycle of burnout, then clarifying your values, prioritizing your life, establishing healthy boundaries, and honoring your limits are all essential to your recovery. Ignore these and you risk falling right back into burnout—often before you have recovered from the previous bout.

1. What values do you aspire to? What values are expressed in how you actually live? As you are beginning to define your core values, how are they different from your aspirational and lived values?

2. What areas of your life are competing for priority? How will you decide which comes first?

3. Is your relationship with God your first priority? How does this affect all your other relationships?

4. Where do you see a need for boundaries in your life? What are the relationships, behaviors, or things that you need to form stronger boundaries around?

5. List some of the minimum and maximum limits in your life that define the playing field for your freedom.

12

BREAKING FREE

L iving in a broken world means that we all will be wounded. Some wounds are self-inflicted, and some are caused by people who didn't intend to hurt us. Other wounds are the result of the brokenness around us. Physical wounds usually heal, though they often leave a scar. Emotional and spiritual wounds don't heal naturally. Tending to our emotional and spiritual pain can cause us to relive it on some level, so facing such deep wounds takes great courage.

The wounds we carry with us shape how we interact with the world. We create defenses to protect ourselves and keep the bad people out. Unfortunately, these defenses keep many good people from entering our lives too. Defense strategies show up as personality traits, generational patterns of behavior in our families, vows we made to ourselves as children, imagined negative responses by people we respect, and interpersonal conflict or defensiveness. No matter what strategies we employ, maintaining these defenses is lonely, exhausting work. In many cases, leaders burn out because they can no longer keep up all their defenses.

In the previous chapters, we discussed how to become whole,

secure, and separate. As you move through recovery, you will work through each of those steps multiple times. Healing from burnout happens in phases and cycles over several years. Each time we grow our sense of wholeness, deepen our identity in God's love, and rediscover our core values, we become a little more resilient and capable of facing our wounds and the wounding world.

In this chapter, we will explore the ways that we are wounded and how to break free from our defensive patterns to live in healthy, courageous vulnerability. However, I need to issue a warning before we move on. If you have suffered trauma or abuse, you should work through these wounds with a licensed, trauma-informed therapist. Some of the steps that follow could do greater damage if your trauma is relived in unsafe ways. Please proceed with caution.

We all need to approach the following steps with the love of Christ. Many burned-out leaders are perfectionists, are self-loathing, or have a strong inner critic. You will need to manage these habits as part of your recovery. For now, try to be gentle and kind with yourself. I find it helpful to approach myself as if I'm helping a scared child (and in many ways, I still am that scared little boy). Using my imagination in this way helps me overcome my own negative self-talk and have empathy and gentleness as I reframe my self-understanding. From my secure position in Christ, I can help the parts of me that are still self-protecting.

BREAK DESTRUCTIVE HABITS

The first step in tearing down our defenses is to identify and eliminate toxic habits and personality traits within ourselves. *Toxic* may be an overused word in American culture, but I think it applies here. We all have personality traits or ways of relating that are poisonous to our relationships. These self-protective parts of our personality either cause us to withdraw from others or drive others away. Both strategies weaken us because we need the love and encouragement that can only be found in healthy relationships. Like drinking fouled water, we think we're quenching our thirst, but we're just making ourselves sick.

What are your negative or toxic personality traits? You are probably aware of some, and I bet you are blind to others. To deal with your blind spots, you need the help of safe people who can gently tell you the truth. However, these people may not trust you to hear them. They may be afraid to speak the truth because of your prior defensiveness or your normal toxic patterns.

You first need to demonstrate your desire to change. Start with what you know needs to change and what you can work on easily. Below is a partial list of issues you may want to explore. For each one ask yourself: "Am I . . . ?"

accusatory	holding a grudge
anxiety filled	inflexible
arrogant	insincere
attention seeking	interrupting
avoiding responsibility	jaded
blaming	jealous
cheating	judgmental
controlling	a know-it-all
critical of others	lacking intimacy
cruel	lacking trust
defensive	lazy
destructively competitive	lying
drama queen/king	manipulative
entitled	mean
elitist	narcissistic
enmeshed with someone	negative
fearful	never wrong
grumpy	not apologizing

passive	selfish
passive aggressive	shame filled
people pleasing	shame driven
a perfectionist	stubborn
self-centered	stuffing negative emotions
self-critical	uncontrolled in my anger
self-loathing	underperforming
self-medicating	

The apostle Paul knew that we couldn't just eliminate sinful or destructive habits from our lives. They need to be replaced with life from the Holy Spirit (see Romans 7 8). When you have identified a toxic personality trait or habit, ask yourself, "What is the opposite characteristic of that trait?" Can you find this in the character of Christ or in the fruit of the Spirit? It's important to replace destructive habits with healthy ones and practice new ways of responding. For example, you can quiet your inner critic and revoice your internal monologue with healthy affirmations of God's love and grace. The promises of God in Scripture are a powerful tool in silencing that inner critic.

Sometimes we need to express negative emotions like anger, grief, and sadness in healthier ways. We can't just replace grief with joy by changing a habit. We must express the grief fully and let it out, which can then lead us to feel the joy of release. Sometimes the way out of the negative emotion is to work through it. However, be gentle with yourself. If working through a negative emotion causes deeper pain, you will want to enlist the help of a qualified therapist. Lament is an immensely helpful spiritual practice in learning to express these negative emotions. We'll explore this practice more in the next chapter. For now, it's important to find ways to feel and express your negative emotions without hurting yourself or others.

Remember our discussion of the true self and false self? In this step we are identifying what is false within us (toxic traits or habits) and what is true within us (grief, sadness, anger). In each case we are bringing these parts of us into our union with Christ. We are letting the Holy Spirit gently lead us into the character of Jesus. This will mean changing some of our core values to be in line with what Jesus teaches and models. As we change those beliefs, our behavior changes too. This doesn't always happen automatically. Sometimes we must do the hard work of replacing bad habits with good self-discipline, especially those habits rooted in generations of negative family scripts and behavior.

RECOGNIZE AND CHANGE NEGATIVE GENERATIONAL PATTERNS

In chapter 3, I introduced the idea that our family of origin has a major impact on our inner life. In this section I want to reintroduce this concept and offer some solutions. Every family has behavioral patterns that we assimilate as we grow. Some are good, some are unhealthy, and some may be destructive. For example, growing up in an abusive household may make one more likely to abuse others as adults—unless the one who was abused sees the problem and chooses to break the cycle. Even the good and healthy things we learn growing up can have a shadow side in our adult lives. As I mentioned earlier, my family focused on academic achievement (good), but that means I can sometimes come across as a know-it-all (shadow). Pete Scazzero, author of *Emotionally Healthy Spirituality*, explains:

> Family patterns from the past are played out in our present relationships without us necessarily being aware of it. Someone may look like an individual acting alone—but they are really players in a larger family system that may go back, as the Bible says, three to four generations. Unfortunately, it is not possible to erase the negative effect of our history. This family history lives inside

all of us, especially in those who attempt to bury it. . . . The price
we pay for this flight is high. Only the truth sets us free.[1]

What destructive behaviors or negative thinking has been passed
down through your family tree? Awareness of these generational
patterns is an important part of healing our relationships—and not
just our family relationships. But how can we identify these patterns
since they were in place long before we entered the world? To discern them, we talk to multiple generations about their experiences
in the family. We then use this information to construct a genogram
(a visual representation of our family relationships). It's like a family
tree but with an added layer of relational information. Here are some
steps to creating a basic genogram.[2]

Start your genogram by drawing your family tree. Include all the
marriages, children, and siblings going back at least three generations
(your parents, your grandparents, and your great-grandparents). A
simple internet search for "genogram symbols" will give you suggestions for how to visually depict these relationships. You may find it
helpful to use genogram software to create this chart. I used GenPro
to help me create mine.[3]

Next, decide what type of information to pursue. For example, if
you were doing a medical genogram, you would ask questions about
health history. For our purposes, we are interested in how the people
in our family relate to one another and to the world around them.
Start by writing down everything you already know, and then craft
questions that will help you uncover the information you need. Here
are some sample questions:

- Tell me about your parents. Can you describe their
  personalities?
- What were your siblings like?
- What do you remember about your grandparents or
  great-grandparents?

- What made your parents happy/sad/angry/depressed?
- How did your parents handle anger/sadness/grief/conflict?
- How did your father relate to women? To other men?
- How did your mother relate to men? To other women?
- What were the clear rules in your family?
- What were the hidden rules in your family?
- Were there broken relationships in your family? Why?
- Were there any patterns of abuse in your family's past?
- Did any of your family members suffer major trauma?
- What did you love about your father/mother/siblings/ grandparents?
- What did you not love about your father/mother/siblings/ grandparents?

Schedule interviews with the adults in your extended family. Start with those closest to you (parents, siblings, grandparents) and then move outward to those who remember earlier generations (aunts, uncles, your grandparents' siblings). It's not necessary to interview everyone, but you'll want to interview enough people to ensure an accurate picture of family patterns. Some may not want to answer your questions. Some families refuse to talk about their negative behaviors, which is itself a negative behavior to notice and change. Give them time and patiently explain what you're trying to do. This isn't about digging up dirt on your family or making anyone look bad. It's about creating a healthier family for the next generation. Don't force anyone to answer your questions. Those who are willing to answer will probably give you enough information to identify generational patterns.

Try to trace these generational patterns through your family tree and write them on the chart. Use different colors or symbols for each pattern. You want to be able to trace them through your family down to you. The goal of this exercise is to look for patterns that carry *across generations* and are still active in your family. Chances are good that these generational patterns are working in you too. Own them as part of your story and start to pay attention to their effects. If you can discover when and why these patterns of behavior started, it will help you to notice them in your own life.

Some negative behaviors you won't be able to change. However, you can usually mitigate their effects if you are aware of them. Other patterns you can change, but it will take hard work. Warning: some of your family members may not like that you are making these changes. As you become healthy, your health may reveal their dysfunction. They may feel like you are judging them and call you self-righteous. Don't take this personally. You have been part of an unhealthy family system your whole life and that system will resist change. There is a good possibility that, with time, your new health will help your extended family too. Be patient. Don't let resistance keep you from pursuing health for you and your children.

After you've done your genogram work, teach what you learned to the next generation. Your children and grandchildren will benefit from your insight. They may even be able to identify patterns in you that you didn't see, so be sure to thank them for the help (even if it stings).

UNCOVER CHILDHOOD VOWS

In the book *Managing Leadership Anxiety*, Steve Cuss defines a child-hood vow as "a promise you made to yourself as a child, either consciously or subconsciously, that informs the way you see and operate in the world."[4] These promises were probably made during a time of pain, stress, or trauma. They are based in *your experience of the event* and may or may not coincide with what actually happened. You formed these vows in reaction to the meaning you assigned to your experience. In the moment, your childhood vows seemed necessary and good for your protection and safety. They probably served you well as a child, giving you tools you needed to protect yourself from the dangers in your world.

As we grow into adulthood, we leave behind things from our childhood. We learn to develop new, more mature ways of relating to others. We grow in strength and resilience and learn how to avoid dangers. Part of this growth is identifying and replacing the child-hood vows that hinder our adult relationships. Because these vows have been a security blanket for most of our lives, they will be hard to let go. However, like with our childhood blankies, if we give them up, the adults in our lives will have greater respect for us.

To identify your childhood vows, listen to your internal self-talk. There are certain phrases that can signal you are functioning under a childhood vow. Here are a few examples of such phrases you may be saying to yourself:

- *I will never* . . . "I will never trust him with my feelings again."
- *I should* . . . "I should not feel this way."
- *Always* . . . "Always give 100 percent."
- *I have to* . . . "I have to appear strong, happy, or intelligent."
- *I must* . . . "I must remain in control."

Listen to your self-talk. Any time it becomes critical or sham-ing, there may be a childhood vow at work in the background. Steve Cuss says, "Identifying and repenting of a childhood vow is a personal experience and is best done with someone you trust: a friend or a therapist."[5] He goes on to suggest writing a letter to repent of your vow and writing out the good promises of Jesus that replace it.

For me, it helped to imagine talking to my childhood self in the moment the vow took place. I praised my younger self for identifying the danger and for being so resourceful, but I also told myself how the way I've been acting is based on a lie. Then I told younger Sean the good news of the new security I've found in Jesus.

Together, the broken child and I made the decision to reject the lie we've been believing and to trust Jesus in this area. Writing all this down as a letter or in a journal can externalize the event and help you approach it more objectively.

I've found it is important to identify the event and the reason I made a childhood vow if that information is available. However, if it isn't accessible, that's okay. The main thing is to clearly identify the vow (the lie we are believing) and how we express it (the negative behavior that flows from it). Once we have identified the lie and the behavior, we can replace the lie with the truth and choose a new behavior based on that.

I used to believe that if someone gave me a gift, I was bound by their wishes in how I used that gift. I told myself, "If you don't do what they want, they will stop liking you and no longer give you gifts." I was letting people manipulate and control me because they gave me something. Then I realized that when Jesus gives a gift, it comes with no strings attached. His gifts are free. He doesn't say, "I will save you from sin if you promise to behave." He recognizes that we cannot be free from sin until he saves us. His salvation changes us from the inside out. God's mercy in Jesus leads us to repent of sinful ways; we don't have to earn his mercy first.

When I realized that a true gift comes with no strings attached, I began receiving gifts that way. I remember the first time I realized someone was giving me a gift to manipulate me. I asked them, "Was this a gift or a manipulation? Because I was under the impression it was a gift. Had I known you would use it to manipulate me, I never would have accepted it." I wish I could describe the freedom and power I felt in that moment. I also wish I could say that the other person received the message well. They didn't. However, they didn't try manipulating me that way again.

In that example, did you spot the vow I had made to myself? What lie was I believing? What truth set me free? How did my behavior change?

SILENCE THE AMPLIFIED VOICES

We all have people in life who exert greater influence on our thinking. People whose opinions we respect naturally have more sway. But sometimes our imagination assigns a person greater influence than they actually carry, and it can feel like they are shouting. Maybe you've assigned such influence to a teacher, coach, religious figure, parent, or spouse. In any given situation you find yourself imagining how they would respond to you, even though in real life they probably wouldn't respond in the way you think. Steve Cuss calls them the giants on our shoulders.

These voices feel loud and critical, but they aren't real. Here's the dirty little secret: *they are your own negative self-talk that you have subconsciously assigned to another person.* There may be something about a person's personality, position, or influence that leads you to connect them as a negative voice, but it's important to realize that they are not saying those words. These amplified voices aren't real.

I occasionally imagine my parents saying something critical to me in the moment. It usually starts by asking myself, "What would your mother say?" or "What would Dad think about that?" I don't know where these questions came from, but I can remember thinking them from childhood. Once I ask the question, I imagine I can hear my parents saying what sounds like things they said in my childhood, but their words are much more critical—sometimes even abusive—and lacking the love that my real parents have for me. When I catch myself doing this, I've learned to ask, "Is Mom or Dad in the room right now?" That's enough to help me realize that I'm engaging in negative self-talk and my imagination is assigning it to a powerful voice in my life whom I respect.

If you can, talk to the real people whose imagined voices have become amplified in your head. Ask their opinion on the matter. What they say in real life never matches what you hear them saying in your imagination. The more you have these conversations with *real people*, the less you will amplify their voices in your head. Those amplified voices are like a mirage in the desert: all we have to do is move toward them with curiosity and they disappear, and we are left with the barren sand of our own negative self-talk. Applying some self-compassion based on the promises of Jesus is like a river of life in these moments.

LEARN TO REMAIN PRESENT IN CONFLICT

Your journey out of burnout will lead you through conflict. To make amends, you may have to revisit the conflicted relationships that led you to burn out in the first place. As you establish boundaries in your life, you will likely face resistance from people who don't know how to relate to your new way of being in the world. Even if you don't face conflict now, chances are you will in the future. Learning to remain present during conflict is an essential skill in your recovery and your work to remain free from future burnout.

Remaining present in conflict means that you have developed the emotional intelligence to identify and regulate your internal responses so you can actively listen and appropriately respond outwardly to the other person. You can control your reactivity, keeping your emotions from infecting them and their emotions from infecting you. This will prevent you from doing something that would sever or injure the relationship.

Remaining present in conflict starts with developing self-awareness. When we feel internal anxiety and fear associated with conflict, we usually have a fight, flight, freeze, or fawn response. In the *fight* response we defend the self by attacking the other person. This can show up as aggression, anger, shouting, or passive-aggressive behavior. The *flight* response is when we run away or hide from the conflict by ignoring, internalizing, avoiding, or denying it. When we *freeze*, we become like a deer in the headlights. We don't know what to do, so we do nothing. This can show up as apathy, indecision, spacing out, or waffling. And when we *fawn*, we let someone run right over us. We give in to their wishes so that we don't have to be assertive. People pleasing, codependency, boundary violation, and lack of self-care can all be fawning responses. Whatever your response, you need to be aware of what is happening in you; recognize your emotions and how they are affecting both yourself and others. This takes practice, so be patient with yourself.

The next step to remaining present in conflict is to regulate your response. Maintaining self-control in the moment is key. You need to maintain trust, but an emotional attack destroys trust. Beware of turning the emotional attack inward. Sometimes we know we can't attack the other person, so we attack our self, which only makes us more reactive. You need to express your emotions without giving the other person reason to fear or become defensive. Be honest but gentle.

Sometimes this is as simple as stating what you're feeling: "I'm feeling angry right now, and I don't want to hurt you. May I have a minute to gather my thoughts?" Other times it means admitting when you have been hurt by others: "What you just said hurt me" or "I don't think you are treating me fairly." These may be followed by a statement that risks trust: "You're a good person, and I don't think that's what you meant to do." Lowering your voice in both tone and volume can help to de-escalate the tension. Be sure your responses sound calm, gentle, and open to the other person. A nonanxious response will do wonders to advance the conversation.

Finally, develop an internal posture of empathy, compassion, and curiosity toward the other person. They may be attacking you simply because you are the nearest target. What's really going on may have nothing to do with you. Be curious about the full reality, not just your experience. What's the story behind their anger? What's going on inside them that led to this conflict? Asking questions about what's happening in their life and how they feel about it may be all that's needed to defuse the conflict. You can't respond with empathy and curiosity if you are wrapped up in your own emotional response. Turn off your emotional autopilot and develop genuine curiosity about other people. By remaining present and relationally connected through the conflict, your anxiety won't cause you do to something you'll regret later.

RESPOND TO CRITICS WITH GRACE

Acting toward others with compassion, empathy, and curiosity will help you understand their motivations and actions. Understanding will allow you to be gracious and loving in the face of anger and opposition. This is especially true when it comes to our critics. Sometimes their words sting because they echo our own inner critic. Rather than becoming defensive when criticized, we need to learn to love our critics by listening to them well. Defensiveness is the false self trying to prop up a lie. Don't assume that your critics are right just because you feel guilt or shame; reserve your evaluation of their words for a time when you can work through your own emotions.

Remain curious about your critic. Thank them for coming to you. Honor the courage it took for them to say these things. Restate their criticism in your own words to make sure you've really understood them and to make them feel heard. Try to discover not only what they mean but what led them to say these things. Get the story behind the story. Ask about their life, their work, and their family. Show that you are genuinely interested in them as a person, even in the face of their criticism. Love them by seeking their good first.

After you have made a relational connection, ask your critic for suggestions about what you could do differently. Thank them for their suggestions, but don't commit to anything. Instead, tell them you'd like to take some time to think through what they've said. Ask if they would be available to answer further questions if you have any. Keep asking questions until they give you something practical. If they can't offer practical advice, this may be a sign that their criticism has nothing to do with you. In that case, it's probably some pain in their lives that they have focused in your direction.

If their criticism warrants a response, give them a time when you will make your decision. Make sure you have sufficient time to work through your emotional response and to evaluate their words as objectively as you can. I've found that I typically need forty-eight hours before I can hear their criticism clearly. I like to give myself plenty of time to calm down, assess their words, and measure my response so it is both gentle and firm. Sometimes I may need to confess that they are right and thank them for their help. Other times I will disagree with their assessment, but I need to say that with love and grace. I often take two to four weeks to prepare my response. Here is one example of how I might respond to a critic:

> Thank you for having the courage to come share your thoughts with me. I'd like to give your words the attention they deserve, so I'll give you my response in a few weeks. Would you be willing to answer any questions that come up during that time?

Having healthy separation from others while remaining relationally connected to them requires the hard work of exploring your inner world and understanding your negative tendencies. It involves repenting of childhood vows and silencing your inner critic, even when it sounds like someone else's voice. You need to be able to identify and regulate your own emotions so that you can be available for others. Developing genuine curiosity about others and their stories, even when you are in conflict with them or when they are criticizing you, will help you respond in love and grace.

The final section of this book is about developing the spiritual maturity to become burnout-proof. For now, here are some questions to help you evaluate your differentiation of self.

1. What destructive patterns do you need to break? Which one will be easiest to address? What is your plan to change this pattern?

2. How will you identify negative generational patterns in your family? What patterns are you already aware of? How will you change the family script for the next generation?

3. What childhood vows are you beginning to notice? What do you need to do to repent of these vows? Which promises of Jesus can you apply to each one?

4. Which voices are amplified in your imagination? Can you put a name and face to each voice? Why do you think your negative self-talk is assigned to that person? What truth can replace that negativity?

5. What do you need to do to become more emotionally aware and self-regulated during conflict? How can you better respond to critics with love and grace? What can you do to develop a genuine curiosity instead of becoming defensive?

PART 3

RESILIENCE AGAINST BURNOUT

13

NEVER BURN OUT AGAIN

Working your way out of burnout is a long journey. The first few months may feel exciting as you learn what you need to change and find hope to move forward. How long will it take before you feel like yourself again? Recovery often depends on the depth of your burnout. It may take three to five years or longer. If you do the work of recovery, you will be different than you were before burnout. Like Jacob's hip injury in Genesis 32:31, your burnout may have lifelong effects. As you lead with a limp, let this injury remind you of the path God has led you down to become healthy.

When you finally feel like yourself again, your joy will return, you will have a sense of direction and hope, and you will be ready to live a productive life once more. You will also have a greater awareness of your limits. One day it will hit you: "I'm joyful, grateful, and energetic—I'm not in burnout anymore!" You will be tempted to think that your burnout journey is over, but it's only just begun. If you go back to your old ways of living before burnout, it won't be long before you burn out again. Your transition into life after burnout is an invitation to a spiritual journey. The final section of this book is about navigating that journey so you never burn out again.

THE JOURNEY BEGINS

In the opening pages of John Bunyan's spiritual classic *Pilgrim's Progress*, the main character, Christian, decides to go on a journey to the Celestial City. He begs his family to join him but eventually sets off on his own. Drawn from Bunyan's experience, this tale is an allegory of the Christian life. The locations in the story, such as the Slough of Despond, the Wicket Gate, Vanity Fair, and House Beautiful, frame the spiritual decisions that Christian must make along the way. The people he meets represent vices or virtues that everyone on a spiritual journey must face. Faithful becomes his trusted traveling companion. Hopeful becomes his friend. Giant Despair tries to trap him in Doubting Castle, where Mr. Despondency is a prisoner. In weaving together his story, Bunyan incorporates elements of spiritual development that are common to every Christian's spiritual biography.

Teresa of Ávila describes this same spiritual journey in her book *The Interior Castle*. Instead of an outward journey moving away from home, Teresa's journey is an inward one exploring the stages of development in the soul. She describes the soul as a castle carved from pure diamond and having many mansions (an old term for apartments or dwellings). As one works through the mansions, they move deeper toward the interior of the castle (soul) and closer to God who is the light at the center. Her story is a metaphor for the journey toward Christlikeness and intimacy with God. However, like in Bunyan's story, our spiritual journey also contains dangers and places we can get stuck.

Both *Pilgrim's Progress* as allegory and *The Interior Castle* as an extended metaphor help us understand the spiritual journey by engaging our imagination. They present powerful images that penetrate the hearts of readers. However, we may so easily become engrossed in the details of the story or the metaphor that we lose the big-picture movements. I highly recommend that you read these wonderful books to inform your spiritual journey. If *Pilgrim's Progress* is a story about a journey and *The Interior Castle* is a picture of the journey, then I want to give you a simple map and a set of directions that includes both landmarks and hazards along the way.

I'm assuming you've been on the journey of faith for a while before you lost your way in the desert of burnout. Jesus said, "Enter through the narrow gate. For wide is the gate and broad is the road that leads to destruction, and many enter through it. But small is the gate and narrow the road that leads to life, and only a few find it" (Matt. 7:13–14). God has opened a way out of this wasteland. Through Jesus, he offers a new path on a narrow road. The desert was a necessary part of your journey. If God didn't bring you here, you would never have seen this humble little path. Now you have the choice to follow the Jesus way and walk the narrow path with him. Your burnout can be redeemed if it leads you to Jesus and his way of living.

Walking through the small gate means beginning a journey you cannot control along the narrow way. The Holy Spirit will help you navigate the twists and turns, the rises and falls, and the difficulty of the trail as he guides you through your story. Each stage in this journey presents different opportunities and obstacles. All God asks is that you follow his lead and depend on his strength.

THE TERRAIN OF THE SPIRITUAL JOURNEY

Over these next few chapters, we will look at the three types of terrain you must travel to develop resilience against burnout. First, we will explore the dark valley of grief and loss through lament. Next, we will view the mountains of the false self. Finally, we will land on the beautiful shore of life as the beloved of God. This journey travels through the terrain created by the pain of your own story and your relationships with God and self. Janet Hagberg says, "If we nurture our spiritual life and experience the healing of life's wounds, especially after age thirty-five, new levels of intuitive, inspired, courageous, and creative leadership will emerge that are unique to our own life's calling."[1] The journey out of the desert wasteland of burnout leads us into a healthy new life and a more dynamic way of leading. It's a journey away from maintaining image and wielding power toward confident but humble leadership rooted in God's love for you in Christ.

When leaders find themselves in the desert of burnout, they know they can't stay, so they make a choice to move. Some retreat from the desert back to the lives they lived before. After a little rest and some minor changes, they return to the life they had before. Eventually these leaders will burn out again. Other leaders see the futility of returning to their old life knowing that they will just burn out again, so they change careers in search of something different. Honestly, this option does work for some, but most who change careers experience shame over giving up on their calling. They feel like quitters. The reason most leaders choose one of these options is because moving forward means experiencing the pain of grief and loss. However, the only way to build resilience is to work through what we most want to avoid.

Leaders usually avoid their grief not because it will hurt but because it will take time. If I could guarantee that the pain would be intense but only last a few days, most leaders would jump at that opportunity. They are willing to suffer a pain for a while to move forward. However, working through grief and loss mean derailing their plans for the foreseeable future. We don't know how long it will take, or how deep the grief will go. Working through grief means surrendering control, and that's a scary thing for most leaders. They would rather change careers than walk through the valley of the shadow of death.

"The shadow of death" comes from Psalm 23, a beloved and often-quoted psalm that offers a good reminder as we begin the journey toward healing, wholeness, and better leadership. On our journey through grief and loss, God does the work. Psalm 23 shows us that God is the active agent in these verses, and we are passive. In fact, the only things we are required to do in the whole psalm are to walk with God and to dwell in his house. The Lord makes us lie down in green pastures, leads us beside still waters, refreshes our souls, comforts us, calms our fears in the dark valley, prepares the table, and anoints our heads. It's his goodness and mercy that follow us all our lives so that we can dwell in his house forever.

The key to working through grief and loss is to enter God's presence by faith, to boldly and honestly express our pain to him, and to let him heal us. We let God lead us through the valley of our own grief and loss, trusting that no matter what we face, he will be with us. We can take comfort in the wisdom, goodness, and love of the Father to see us through the pain. The Bible even shows us how to do this through the process of lament.

LAMENT

People in burnout talk about feelings of hopelessness, numbness, or grief. All of these expressions communicate that something has been lost, whether it be purpose, vision, or energy. This sense of loss can be hard to discern because it's mixed with other feelings like anger, doubt, frustration, and fatigue. As I said earlier, burnout involves a loss of self. That experience may feel like we are being abandoned by God, but we are not alone. God gives us biblical testimony to show how to handle loss, anger, grief, and other negative emotions. These witnesses can be found in the psalms of lament.

Bible scholars say that the psalms of lament make up between one-third and one-half of the book of Psalms. What kind of pain and loss are you experiencing? I bet there's a psalm for it.

Are you . . .	*Read:*
Sick?	Psalms 28 and 38
Lonely or isolated?	Psalm 25
Losing patience?	Psalms 35 and 79
Feeling abandoned by God?	Psalm 12
Suffering?	Psalms 69–71
Seeking vengeance?	Psalm 137
Being treated unjustly?	Psalms 43 and 109
Desperate?	Psalm 80
Afraid of death?	Psalm 26
Feeling completely hopeless or forgetting God?	Psalm 88
Grieving?	Psalm 55
Experiencing guilt?	Psalm 51
Anguished?	Psalm 6
Confused?	Psalm 22
Depressed?	Psalm 42
Persecuted?	Psalm 3

Learning to lament is an essential step in our spiritual development. Too often we avoid lament because we fear how it will surface. We tell ourselves that we can't lament or that we won't go there. When we feel like God is distant or absent, he's often hiding behind our can'ts and won'ts. When there are painful events in our past that we can't revisit or parts of ourselves that we won't allow into the light, God remains hidden until we are willing to work through the pain. It's not that God is hiding from us; we are putting up a wall that is separating us from God and his healing presence. God is already present in these places from our past, in these parts of our stories, in our souls. He knows them better than we do. Maybe that's what bothers us; maybe we are avoiding God so we don't have to see ourselves in pain.

As I was working through burnout, I discovered an interesting paradox: *the more I tried to avoid my pain, the heavier it became.* All our emotions are connected. Denying one emotion means diminishing access to the others—including the good ones. That's why we feel so numb. As I denied my pain, I also experienced less joy in my life. Artificially reducing grief reduces joy. Expressing grief honestly opens us up to joy. Lament is our pathway into the goodness and joy of God. Failure to lament infects our good and joyous times with the stench of bitterness. A friend of mine told me, "Lament is a place where I can put all this s—t." I think his strong language is warranted here because it expresses the raw emotion and nastiness of what he is experiencing. Lament is the process of mucking out the stalls of our soul. When we fail to lament, we carry that excrement with us. No wonder life stinks.

Lament is the process of letting go of what we have already lost. It requires space to allow our emotions to come to the surface. We need to feel the pain and express it honestly, so lament cannot be forced or rushed, and it will be intensely personal. No one can tell you how to lament. It can be like a child either crying in their father's arms or struggling against their mother's embrace: both are lament. Lament cannot be scheduled or programmed. We practice creating space for it to happen, and we give ourselves permission to lament when the time is right. However, there are some elements in lament that may be helpful for us to keep in mind in the moment.

1. Lament Is Directed toward God

Because lament is directed toward God, it is an expression of faith in God. Almost every psalm of lament moves toward hope or faith in God. Even Psalm 88, the only psalm that does not end in hope, is directed toward God. It's a statement that things are not right in this world made by a good God. Some laments are desperate cries to God: "How long?" "Where are you?" Others turn from cries of pain to songs of worship. To truly lament we must know God is faithful and good—otherwise why cry to him at all?

2. Lament Is Honest

Every lament contains a complaint. That doesn't mean whining about the situation but rather honestly expressing the raw emotion of the moment. A complaint is a cry to God that things are not the way they should be; for example, the righteous are being treated unjustly or the wicked are prospering. It asserts that the current situation is an affront to God's good character. His image bearers are not showing his mercy, love, or goodness; his creation is not demonstrating his righteous glory but is instead evil and destructive. Complaint starts down in the very depths of the soul, and like the keening heard during times of mourning in the Middle East, it erupts in a loud groaning and wailing to God. Laments are volcanic in nature: raw, explosive emotion delivered with powerful language that holds nothing back.

3. Lament States That God Hears or Will Hear

Lament isn't just a complaint to God; it's a cry for justice and an expression of trust in God. Not only does God hear, but he listens deeply and understands the heart of our cry. Maybe this is what David meant when he said, "Before a word is on my tongue you, LORD, know it completely." (Ps. 139:4). God knows us better than we know ourselves. This affirmation phase of a lament demonstrates trust that God hears, understands, and perhaps even identifies with our complaint.

4. Lament Moves to a Specific Petition or Request

Sometimes this can be implied or stated as part of the complaint earlier in the lament. Here we have an opportunity to strongly request—almost demand—that God do something. Basing the request in the character of God, the one lamenting tells God that these conditions cannot last if God is who he claims to be. The lament lays the blame at the feet of God and says, "Your goodness demands that you do something!"

5. Lament Recalls That God Is Indeed Good

As a lament moves toward resolution, we recount the faithfulness of God in the past and again express trust that God has heard our cry. This doesn't mean that the conflict is over, but all our rage, grief, and despair have been spent. All that's left is the love of God for us, his children. The goodness of God and his faithful character outlast our raw emotion. God exhausts our complaint and remains present, loving, and understanding through it all. He has not become defensive, retaliatory, or angry with us. He is big enough to take all our rage and secure enough not to blame us for being honest with him. He knows we are groaning over the brokenness caused by sin, and he is waiting patiently for his time to make all things right again.

Having spent our emotion and received the love of God as we lament, the only right response is worship. The psalms of lament end with some of the most beautiful expressions of praise and hope in the Bible, and the sharp contrast between complaint and worship makes them even more beautiful. In Psalm 7, for example, David calls on God to deliver him and to arise in anger and crush his enemies. David then asks God to vindicate his righteous actions and kill the wicked. This psalm is a desperate cry for God to act, but it ends with these words of praise in verse 17: "I will give thanks to the LORD because of his righteousness; I will sing the praises of the name of the LORD Most High."

Here are some movements that you can make to help you lament:

- Create space for your emotions to surface by entering silence and solitude for an extended time.
- Turn your attention to the reality of God's presence and become aware of his fatherly love.
- Ask the Holy Spirit to help you lament and let the Spirit do his work in his time.
- Be patient with yourself.
- When the time is right, be emotionally honest. Don't edit your words and don't hold back. God already knows how you feel better than you do. Speak the raw truth of what you feel to God.
- Hold on to God in faith. Don't let your grief or sorrow cause you to forget God's character. You may find it necessary to remind yourself of God's holiness, righteousness, goodness, kindness, compassion, patience, and love.
- Make your request to God. What is the deepest cry of your soul? In your honesty, boldly tell God what you need.
- Worship God, knowing that he will be faithful to all his promises.

Sometimes we can't give words to our lament. This is especially true in people who have suffered abuse or other trauma. If you can't express how you feel in words, open your heart to the Holy Spirit in wordless sighs, groaning, or simple silence. Trust that "the Spirit helps us in our weakness. We do not know what we ought to pray for, but the Spirit himself intercedes for us through wordless groans" (Rom. 8:26).

In our experience of burnout, we need to lament. We need to honestly express our anger, call out injustice, and grieve our losses in the presence of our Father God. Think about your burnout. Are you angry? What is at the root of this anger? Is your anger hiding another emotion, such as grief? What has burnout cost you, and what have you lost in the process? Bring these things to God in lament.

Explore your hidden pain as well. What are you afraid to revisit? Which parts of you are you keeping hidden? Find a Christian counselor or a mature, trustworthy friend who can help you realize God's healing presence in the pain. Lament opens us up to receive the love of God again.

> But let all who take refuge in you be glad;
>   let them ever sing for joy.
> Spread your protection over them,
>   that those who love your name may rejoice in you.
> Surely, Lord, you bless the righteous;
>   you surround them with your favor as with a shield.
>   (Ps. 5:11–12)

RECEIVE GOD'S LOVE

One of the hardest things for burned-out leaders is believing that God loves them. Some of these leaders are so defeated or have such negative self-talk that they reject the idea that God could love them. In doing so they are rejecting the gospel, which says that even though they feel unworthy, Christ has made them worthy. If you are going to become burnout-proof, *you will have to learn how to meaningfully and genuinely apply God's love to yourself.*

Think of yourself as a carpenter tending to the rot of a crumbling house. You have wounds that need to be healed. Some of those wounds have been festering for a long time and may have contributed to your burnout. Some may be new, caused by the events just before and during your burnout. Before restoration can begin, you must remove the decay and crumbling parts that are contributing to the problem. Unhealthy beliefs, childhood vows, and family scripts are all part of this rot. The process of removing the decay is *deconstruction*, which opens us up to God's healing power of *reconstruction*.

It's important to remember that God is the healer of our souls; he is the master builder. Our part in this process is to follow his lead.

Deconstruction starts with prayer and is, itself, an act of lament. Psalm 139 has been the most healing passage for me. As I meditate on that psalm, I become more aware of God's presence and of how it's useless to try hiding from him. I'm reminded that he knows me better than I know myself and that he is concerned with righteousness and justice. God is intimately involved in shaping the days of my life to make me like Christ. This gives me the courage to pray like David, "Search me, God, and know my heart; test me and know my anxious thoughts. See if there is any offensive way in me" (Ps. 139:23–24). Praying this prayer honestly is hard. We would rather avoid knowing these grievous things, so we have to start by asking God to give us the desire to be honest about ourselves.

When the Holy Spirit does his convicting work in our hearts, we experience a keen sense of loss as we let go. We need to remember to lament as we deconstruct. Here are some things leaders in burnout often must release to God:

- Let go of our spiritual ego. We need to stop seeing ourselves as being in control of spiritual outcomes and put away the idea that success depends on us and our work.
- Deconstruct our false views of God that are inconsistent with how God describes himself in Scripture. Sometimes this means challenging what we have been taught to believe in church.
- Let go of our false views of self, including any negative, self-critical patterns. This may mean rethinking our understanding of sin and judgment. Brokenness can no longer be our identity.
- Give up our people pleasing, our desire for affirmation, and our need to prove ourselves to others. These are all attempts at self-creation rooted in the false self.
- Surrender dreams, plans, or ideals that drive us but are also the source of frustration.

As we deconstruct the things that are not from God, we will lament their loss because they have been part of us for so long. This frees us to find new hope in different ways of being with God.

Reconstruction is movement toward surrender to God's purposes in our lives. Just as we must think critically for deconstruction—evaluating everything by God's revelation—so too must we think critically for reconstruction. If we don't rebuild our lives on a solid foundation, the whole thing will come crashing down in burnout again. So we turn to God and experience his healing presence as we meditate on his Word—especially his declarations of love for us and his promises for us in Jesus Christ.

- We surrender our spiritual ego and receive the reality that all spiritual outcomes are ultimately from God. The branch (you) bears fruit because of the vine (Jesus). God gives the increase (1 Cor. 3:5–7).
- We surrender our false views of God that are based in our childhood vows, our relationship with our parents, and the misguided teaching we've heard. We receive the character of God modeled by Jesus by allowing our hearts to be formed by his ways.
- We rebuild our view of self by recognizing our original goodness and the fact that what was lost because of sin is being restored because of Christ. We begin to trust the new heart within us as we walk by the Spirit.
- We return to our identity in Christ and renounce all false identities or attempts to self-create. Instead, we receive who the Holy Spirit is shaping us to be and embrace our unique expression of the image of Christ in our gifts, talents, and experience.
- We let go of our desired outcomes and simply follow God. We adopt a slow, unhurried way of being in the world, a way of peace and confidence in God instead of frantic drivenness and hurry.

As we make these movements of deconstruction and reconstruction, it's important to recognize that we are tearing down what is false and God is building in us what is true. We are not the builders. God uses others to build us up, but he is the true master builder. If we are to move through grief and loss, we must learn to lament, deconstruct what is not of God, and dwell in his healing presence as he rebuilds us. This is not an easy process. In fact, it's about to get harder as we face the obstacles to wholeness put up by our false self. From here we move out of the valley and begin to cross the mountains.

1. When you think about leaving the desert of burnout, which option is the most tempting to you: to return to your previous life, to quit on your calling and change careers, or to move through the pain toward healing and wholeness? Which sounds the hardest? Why?

2. What losses have you suffered that could contribute to burnout?

3. What reservations do you have about practicing lament? In what ways does the practice of lament feel like an invitation from God?

4. How does the character of God—his love, goodness, faithfulness, and kindness—create a safe space for you to grieve and lament your losses?

5. In what ways do you need to receive and experience the love of God?

14

SURRENDER TO GOD

The first two times I went through low-grade burnout, I made some minor changes to my life, and I felt good again for a while. Then I went back to my old ways of living and leading. But I was only treating the symptoms and not the disease, so eventually my symptoms returned. Here's the hard lesson I had to learn: *if we don't get to the root cause of our burnout, we will burn out again and again.*

In the depths of my third burnout cycle, the worst one by far, I realized that I was barely surviving. Each experience was worse than the one before. If I entered burnout again, it could kill me. Something had to change.

As I researched burnout and read the stories of other burned-out pastors, I slowly came to realize that changing my work and life patterns would not be enough. I had to change *me*. If I were going to become burnout-proof, I would have to undergo a transformation of the heart. Only as my heart changed would the rest of my life change too.

In earlier chapters, I introduced the false self as an image we project to the world. It has been influenced by our childhood, religious teaching, and the sinfulness we've encountered in ourselves and others. A quick review may be helpful here. In childhood, we develop behaviors designed to help us feel safe. We learn ways to protect ourselves from harm or secure a sense of love and belonging. These patterns that helped us in childhood become unhealthy in our adult years. People pleasing, codependency, and shame-based manipulation often start during our early years. Unhealthy religious structures that value righteous performance over relationships can reinforce these behaviors. Churches that become obsessed with purity before God become harsh and controlling environments where love must be earned. However, it's not easy to detect this church culture. It's usually subtly hidden behind language of grace, faithfulness, and unity.

As we work through our grief and loss and begin to deconstruct our false beliefs, we slowly begin to realize that our false self is part of the problem. We have been complicit in our own deception. Now we must dismantle the false image we've been projecting all our lives. This feels like a monumental task. It's as if the dark valley of grief is opening to reveal an imposing mountain range that seems impossible to cross.

THE MOUNTAINS OF SELF

Here we enter the second and most dangerous phase of our journey. This mountain range we now face represents our internal resistance to the will of God. It's our self-will, and we've built it up through years and years of resistance. Every time we've failed to submit to God, we've pushed the peaks higher and higher. Our will has created the Rocky Mountains of good intentions, desires to honor God, and kingdom building that have conflicted with God's ways all along.

The reason we can't go over, under, or around them is because *these mountains are in us!* We can't just ignore them because we carry them with us wherever we go. The mountains represent the internal defenses built by our false self. Our attempts to prop up our own ego—to maintain the facade that we are good, strong, capable, and independent—just build a barrier between God and us. Crossing these mountains will be a battle of wills. Now God is giving us a choice: submit to his will and let him lead us to the promised land, or keep wandering in the desert we've created for ourselves. If we are to be healthy and whole, God must win.

Going back to Romans 1:25, we "exchanged the truth about God for a lie, and worshiped and served created things rather than the Creator." Whenever we construct a lie, we need a way to keep the truth out. However, Jesus has a way of getting past our defenses. When we first came to faith, he opened our eyes to our resistance to God. Since that time, the Holy Spirit has been guiding us into deeper levels of submission to God. Now, at the base of these mountains, the Spirit is revealing the root of our problem and calling us to total surrender to God's will so we can discover the true freedom we've been missing.

Looking up at these massive mountains is terrifying. We feel so small, and many people are overcome by the enormity of the task. "How can I traverse such daunting terrain?" they ask. Thinking it's impossible, or still overly attached to their self-will, they walk away. Jesus once encountered such a man:

> As Jesus started on his way, a man ran up to him and fell on his knees before him. "Good teacher," he asked, "what must I do to inherit eternal life?"
>
> "Why do you call me good?" Jesus answered. "No one is good—except God alone. You know the commandments: 'You shall not murder, you shall not commit adultery, you shall not steal, you shall not give false testimony, you shall not defraud, honor your father and mother.'"
>
> "Teacher," he declared, "all these I have kept since I was a boy."

Jesus looked at him and loved him. "One thing you lack," he said. "Go, sell everything you have and give to the poor, and you will have treasure in heaven. Then come, follow me."

At this the man's face fell. He went away sad, because he had great wealth (Mark 10:17–22).

Notice how Jesus pokes holes in the man's defenses and gets to the truth of his resistance. This rich man knows the commandments and has kept them since youth. However, Jesus points out that he isn't really keeping the greatest commandment of them all—to love the Lord your God with all your heart, soul, mind, and strength. Jesus asks the man to do the one thing that would demonstrate he loves God more than anything else. He tells the man to give everything he has to the poor. Jesus brings the rich man to the base of his resistance, and the man walks away disheartened and sorrowful. Mark doesn't tell us what happened to the man after he walked away because he wants us to feel the impossibility of the moment and hear Jesus say, "With man this is impossible, but not with God; all things are possible with God" (Mark 10:27).

Surrendering our wills requires the miraculous power of God. We can become so overwhelmed with the difficulty of letting go that, like the rich man, we walk away in grief and sorrow. When we refuse to surrender, God allows us to continue in our struggle. We feel trapped or stuck. God seems absent, uncaring, or capricious. Some people walk away from faith altogether. Perhaps this is what the author of Hebrews meant when he said, "It is impossible for those who have once been enlightened, who have tasted the heavenly gift, who have shared in the Holy Spirit, who have tasted the goodness of the word of God and the powers of the coming age and who have fallen away, to be brought back to repentance" (6:4–6).

We may walk away from the mountains of self for a time, but we will soon find ourselves staring up at them again. We can't escape what's within us. These mountains of self-will must be rejected, or we may reject faith to maintain our self-will. As Jesus said, we cannot serve two masters. We can get stuck here if we have a strong ego, struggle with self-loathing, are filled with guilt or shame, are overly intellectual, are a driven person, or if we become overly focused on doctrine (as in 1 Cor. 13:2).[1]

Pastors and other spiritual leaders often get stuck when faced with their self-will. When your church expects you to be above reproach (1 Tim. 3:2), admitting you've been living from your false self seems like career suicide. Pastors need to build trust with their people by admitting their limits and struggles regularly. Pastors need to be human, just like the rest of us. The permission to be human is one of the greatest gifts a church can give their pastor.

Do you find yourself facing the decision to either radically submit to God or walk away? What resistance are you experiencing in this place? Are you ready to face your false self and to surrender your self-will?

PASSING THROUGH THE MOUNTAINS OF SELF

If these mountains represent our self-will and resistance to God and his ways, then the only way through is total surrender, fully submitting to God's will. Now you might be thinking, "That's impossible! No one can fully submit to God, at least not in this life." Maybe it is impossible to fully submit to God all at once. However, we are not being asked to dismantle everything, only the areas that the Holy Spirit brings to our awareness. He will gently lead us one step at a time.

There is only one way through these mountains: Jesus himself. Jesus said, "I am the way and the truth and the life. No one comes to the Father except through me" (John 14:6). We must abide in him and follow his example by faith, relying on the power of the Holy Spirit and waiting for God to do a miraculous work in our hearts. The way through is the cruciform way, the way of Jesus. This way of the cross begins in a garden.

We can't muscle our way through, think our way through, or rely on our gifts to get us through. Our own strength is what got us here in the first place. To find the transformation that will keep us from ever burning out again, we must begin with prayer. Jesus teaches us this prayer in the garden of Gethsemane.

> Then Jesus went with his disciples to a place called Gethsemane, and he said to them, "Sit here while I go over there and pray." He took Peter and the two sons of Zebedee along with him, and he began to be sorrowful and troubled. Then he said to them, "My soul is overwhelmed with sorrow to the point of death. Stay here and keep watch with me."
>
> Going a little farther, he fell with his face to the ground and prayed, "My Father, if it is possible, may this cup be taken from me. Yet not as I will, but as you will."
>
> Then he returned to his disciples and found them sleeping. "Couldn't you men keep watch with me for one hour?" he asked Peter. "Watch and pray so that you will not fall into temptation. The spirit is willing, but the flesh is weak."
>
> He went away a second time and prayed, "My Father, if it is not possible for this cup to be taken away unless I drink it, may your will be done."
>
> When he came back, he again found them sleeping, because their eyes were heavy. So he left them and went away once more and prayed the third time, saying the same thing (Matt. 26:36–44).

Notice the prayer Jesus repeats three times: "Not as I will, but as you will." Jesus is praying a prayer of submission to the Father over and over. Ignatius of Loyola called this the prayer for holy indifference, and Ruth Haley Barton describes it in *Strengthening the Soul of Your Leadership*:

We need to also pray for *indifference*. This is not the kind of indifference that we associate with apathy; rather, it is the prayer that we would be indifferent to everything but the will of God. . . . As Danny Morris and Charles Olsen put it: "God's will, nothing more, nothing less, nothing else."

The prayer for indifference can be a very challenging prayer for us to pray. . . . It takes time, and often a death to self is required before we can see God's will taking shape in our lives. Here we ask ourselves the question, *What needs to die in me in order for the will of God to come forth?*[2]

We can't develop this holy indifference on our own. We need the miraculous work of the Holy Spirit to transform our hearts. With Jesus we pray, "Not as I will, but as you will," and we continually repeat this prayer in God's presence. We can't hurry this process. We must trust in the slow work of God. As the Holy Spirit strips away the power of our false self, and out emerges our true self made in God's image, it can feel like death. As we follow Jesus down this path of indifference to everything but God's will, we follow him to the cross and into the tomb.

This dismantling of our self-will means asking the Holy Spirit to reveal the parts of ourselves that are not submitted to him. This exploration is painful. We don't like seeing or acknowledging the truth of our resistance to God. However, the pain of the cross illuminates the way of Christ for us. We must be willing to endure the pain of conviction, to agonize and lament over our separation from God, and to commit ourselves to him. Then we enter the waiting of the grave.

In the tomb with Christ, we learn patience to wait on God's work. The grave is not a peaceful place of rest; it's a place of violent transformation. Like a caterpillar in its cocoon, we are being made into something altogether different. Think of the radical changes inside that chrysalis: most of the caterpillar's body dissolves and a whole new body grows. In the same way, radical changes are occurring in our hearts as we wait upon the Lord. The painful work of healing and restoration has begun.

Here in the tomb, the Holy Spirit is transforming us from self-willed people into people who are filled with God's will and his unconditional love for the world in Christ Jesus. Here we learn to accept our humanity with its weakness, limitations, and brokenness. As we wait for God to do his work of transformation, we sit in God's love and soak up all that is good and true for us in Christ. We no longer need to be driven for affirmation and praise from others. Who we are in Christ is enough. We are the beloved. We are becoming who we were always meant to be—image bearers of God.

To create the space necessary for this work of transformation, we disconnect from the world through silence and solitude. We return to silence again and again until holy indifference becomes real in us. To the outside world, this cocooning in the tomb looks like self-centeredness. As we withdraw from service and say no to everything but God, it may seem like we are checking out, but we are coming to life. The resurrection of our true self begins slowly.

I don't think it's possible to become whole without time alone in God's healing presence. As we sit in silence and solitude, we create space for the parts of us that need to be healed to come to the surface. Here we are safe to notice our wounds and defensive strategies and to offer them to God. In the tomb we are letting go of all that is not God. Every love that could get in the way must be released. In this place of silence, we experience the darkness of death as we let go of our family, friends, work, self-pride, false identities, need for affirmation, and more. Everything is stripped away until we are naked and unafraid in the presence of God once again. When God is our only love, we begin to learn how to love others.

We emerge from traversing the mountains of self as we emerge from the tomb—when we have new life within. When our prayers for holy indifference are answered, and we truly desire God's will alone, we know our resurrection day has come. We now genuinely believe that we are the beloved of God, and we no longer have to search for love anywhere else. No longer are we driven toward success. No longer do we feel the need prove ourselves to others. We have surrendered control and outcomes. We are complete in God. As we emerge from the tomb, God clothes our nakedness in the radiance of his love. In this place of belovedness, this new garden of resurrection, God teaches us to love others with his love. No longer self-willed, we are learning to love others self-sacrificially.

THE OTHER SIDE

Everything is different on the other side of the mountains. We emerge into the promised land, where we are healed, whole, and free. This journey has taught us that only one will can win and that to experience true freedom we must fully surrender to God's will. We only thought we were free in our self-will, but we were actually getting ourselves stuck deeper in the mud. Our freedom became our prison. Now we have learned that by surrendering to God's will and becoming captive to his desires, we experience joy and freedom like never before. It isn't a delusion; rather, we are seeing clearly for the first time. Now the life of Christ within us—that is, our Spirit-led self—draws us forward into new stages of faith. As C. S. Lewis described it in *The Last Battle*, "I have come to home at last! This is my real country! I belong here. This is the land I have been looking for all my life, though I never knew it till now. . . . Come farther up, come farther in!'"[3] We have come home at last. From now on we move farther up and farther in God's love.

Burnout doesn't happen on this side of the mountains. It *can't* happen. Remember what led to burnout? Anxiety, stress, control, unmet expectations, frustrated dreams, negative self-talk, loss of self. When we fully submit to the will of God and live securely in his love, such things are impossible. Only when we forget God's love or regress into self-will do they again take over. Our anxiety, stress, and negative self-talk are swallowed up in Christ's love and power.

If you want to work your way to surrender, start by finding a place of silence and solitude where you can be alone in the presence of God. You may want to get away for a prayer retreat to begin this process. I like to send pastors away with their spouse for a week-long retreat where they have plenty of time for silence and solitude. They usually tell me that it takes three full days before their hearts and minds settle enough to begin hearing the still, small voice of the Spirit. However, the real work happens day by day as you spend regular time in silence and solitude, submitting yourself to God and listening for his voice.

As your resistance begins to surface, expect some nasty feelings along with it. Anger, grief, and even depression can accompany the death of the false self's influence. Allow yourself to feel these emotions and bring them to God in faith-filled lament. Don't shame or judge yourself. Let the Spirit do his healing work as he breaks down your resistance.

Now sit in the love of God for you in Christ. Meditate on your unity with Jesus and what it means to be "in Christ." Stay there until your identity as the beloved of God gives you a sense of calm security in the arms of your loving Father.

Secure in God's love for you, surrender to him. Let his will become your own, and then move out into the world with sacrificial love that flows from your heart.

Go slowly. God is never in a hurry. Jesus didn't feel rushed, and you don't have to either. Wait upon the Lord, and he will renew your strength.

1. What resistance do you feel toward the work of surrendering your will to God?

2. What are the things (internal attitudes, external attachments, etc.) that pushed your mountains of resistance higher? What is God inviting you to surrender to him?

3. Write yourself a note of encouragement to help you face your false self.

4. Which spiritually mature people in your life can help you discern what you need to do to stop living from your false self?

5. Write a kind and gentle letter to your false self, letting it know it won't be needed any more. Be detailed and specific about the nature of this false self and the characteristics of your true self in Christ that will replace it.

15

LOVING LIFE

few years ago we left our home of eighteen years to move back to
Grand Rapids, Michigan. My wife had the opportunity to pursue
her dream job, and I was ready to give myself to helping pastors full-time. The housing market in Grand Rapids was crazy. Houses were selling for well above their asking price and they only lasted a few days on the market. We were moving from a rural community that had not yet fully recovered from the 2008 housing market crash into a market that was one of the hottest in the country. So we bought a house that needed some work. We decided that I would take a few months to remodel the kitchen before starting my new ministry.

The first night in a new house is strange. Everything smells different, there are noises that you aren't yet accustomed to, and almost all your belongings are still in boxes. In fact, we had arrived so late, that the only things we unpacked were our mattresses and bedding and the coffee maker (which wouldn't fit under the kitchen cabinets). I went to sleep thinking about all the work we had to do. Move in, build cabinets, demo kitchen, drywall, electrical, etc. It took me a while to get to sleep.

After a long night, I awakened slowly. The lights and noise from the street had awakened me several times in the night. I was sore from loading the truck the day before, and the coffee wasn't ready yet. I was excited about the possibilities of a new day, but I was still in a mental fog from last night's sleep. As we sipped our morning brew, our friends and family arrived to help unload the truck. Within a few minutes the, house was buzzing with activity, and I was awake and engaged in our new life.

Emerging from the mountains of self, landing on the beautiful shore of our life as the beloved in Christ, our journey is a process of slowly arriving. Up to this point we have been self-willed. We've lived each day according to our own desires and under our own control. We may have thought we were following God, but this experience has taught us differently. Now we know how it feels to surrender to God's will and God's ways. As we enter this phase of our journey, we are learning how to live as someone surrendered to God because of his love instead of living from self-will. Everything is different.

BEGINNER'S MINDSET

As we learn to live as the beloved of God, it's important to develop a beginner's mindset that frees us from the need to prove ourselves. We are learning to believe and live as one who is accepted by God. We've just had the humbling experience of coming face to face with our false self. Now we know that the Father loves us, we are united to the Son, and the Holy Spirit is shaping us into his image. This security of our adoption gives us quiet confidence and honest curiosity about God, life, and others.

As we explore the changes that take place as the beloved of God, you may be thinking they sound too good to be true. What I'm presenting may feel like an unrealistic ideal; therefore, please hear these two words of caution.

First, don't get so caught up in the ideal that you get frustrated by your present level of growth. We are just beginning to express this new sense of our belovedness at its most basic level. As we go deeper into God's love for us, we become more fully like Christ. It's not up to you to grow yourself into the perfect image of Christ. That's the Holy Spirit's job. He will work at whatever pace he deems best. Rather than focusing on the ideal, look for the present fruit of the Spirit's work. I've heard it said that the happiest people focus on the journey, not the destination. I believe you will be much more joyful if you are giving thanks for what God has already done in you than if you focus on what is missing from your character.

Second, don't give up hope that this spiritual maturity will be yours. It may seem like an unrealistic ideal, and if it were merely up to you, it would be impossible. Do you remember the scene from Mark 10:17–31, when the rich young ruler came to talk to Jesus? I'm amazed at how it plays out. After Jesus tells him about the commandments, the man says, "All these I have kept since I was a boy." Then Mark tells us, "Jesus looked at him and loved him." Jesus is about to deliver a devastating blow. He's going to tell this man the one thing he doesn't want to hear. Jesus understands the man and speaks directly to the part of him that isn't fully surrendered to God. This is love. Jesus says, "One thing you lack. . . . Go, sell everything you have and give to the poor, and you will have treasure in heaven. Then come, follow me."

At first this sounds like four things: (1) go, (2) sell, (3) come, and (4) follow. However, it's really one thing. Jesus is pointing out the commandment the man hasn't followed, the command to have no other gods. Jesus is effectively saying, "The one thing you lack is to love God more than everything else." Jesus's message was loud and clear because we're told, "At this the man's face fell. He went away sad, because he had great wealth." He was unwilling to love God more than everything else. This is a hard text. What would we do if Jesus said this to us? Is he saying this to us? Notice how the disciples respond in verses 23–26:

> Jesus looked around and said to his disciples, "How hard it is for the rich to enter the kingdom of God!"
>
> The disciples were amazed at his words. But Jesus said again, "Children, how hard it is to enter the kingdom of God! It is easier for a camel to go through the eye of a needle than for someone who is rich to enter the kingdom of God."
>
> The disciples were even more amazed, and said to each other, "Who then can be saved?"

You may identify with the disciples: it seems impossible! In their ancient Jewish culture, the disciples were taught that God rewards the righteous with riches; therefore, a rich man must be more righteous than anyone. Then Jesus tells them it will be hard for this man to enter the kingdom of God. The disciples don't understand. Surely this man was part of the kingdom. If he's not in, then no one has hope. But Jesus responds by saying, "With man this is impossible, but not with God; all things are possible with God" (Mark 10:27).

CONTINUING SURRENDER TO GOD

Going through the dark valley of grief and loss we had to turn inward so we could be healed. We needed to grieve, lament, and experience God's love for us. To do this, we withdrew from outward acts of service, which often were attempts to earn something from God or others. This inward movement started us down the path that leads to confronting the mountains of our false self and helped us find strength to go through it.

Going through the deconstruction of self-will by following

Jesus through the garden, the cross, and the grave prepares us for resurrection to a new way of living. Now we *desire* to follow God's will. As we learn to live in the knowledge of our belovedness in Christ, continually surrendering our self-will to God's will, something amazing happens: our hearts naturally turn outward in love for our neighbor. Serving others is no longer a chore or duty but the joy of our heart. However, our service will look very different than it did in before burnout. Back then we were looking for acceptance, we were driven and busy, we fell into people pleasing, and we allowed others to define success for us (usually in unhealthy, needy ways). We were fed by the needs of the false self. We were driven to prove ourselves to God and others. Maintaining the facade we thought others would accept was exhausting.

Here, in living from our belovedness, life looks and feels very different because we start from the reality that we are accepted by God. We are secure in Christ, and nothing can take us from the Father's love. God's faithful, covenant love, goodness, wisdom, power, and presence form the foundation for our submission to his will. In Christ, God accepts us just as we are, but by his Holy Spirit he is shaping us to be like Christ—our true self. Our full acceptance by God changes the way we live.

On the beautiful shore of God's love, life at a frantic or driven pace no longer makes sense. That habit may still pull at you, but now you seek quietude—an archaic word often used to describe a peaceful scene like a still pond or an undisturbed field. Personal quietude is a state of inner stillness, calm, or peace. Our drivenness, inner turmoil, and self-loathing are beginning to fade as they are replaced by peaceful awareness that we are beloved by God.

As we follow God's will, we watch his example and adjust to his pace. *God is never in a hurry.* When we follow God and let him shape our priority, our lives become unhurried too. Contentment starts to permeate our souls as we begin to see all of life, even our struggles and losses, as a gift from God. When we experience security in God's love for us, we become less reactive; we are no longer easily offended or defensive. We are becoming unflappable and more able to roll with whatever life brings. Knowing we are secure in Christ brings a stability to our lives that frees us to move toward others in ways we would have previously considered too risky. Instead of seeking affirmation and acceptance from others, now we are offering community and genuine love for our neighbors. We are learning to love life in community as God intended it to be.

People may need a while to adjust to our new way of love. Be patient with them. They are still looking for the person they knew before our burnout—someone driven to succeed and earn acceptance. Now we may no longer follow the usual paths of ministry and service. As we worked through lament and surrender, we gained clarity or a new sense of calling. We now shape our vocation or ministry by who we really are instead of who others think we should be. We comfortably lean into our gifts, talents, and strengths as uniquely given by God. Our experience shapes what we do as we now have wisdom to bring to bear on life.

Ministries often come from wounds. As we find healing and wholeness, we will want to help others walk the same path. We are being drawn forward by love and wholeness instead of by need and insecurity. This gives us a profound freedom to say no to things that others think we should be doing. Our experience has given us the security to live another way. Our God-centered orientation has opened us to loving compassion that acts differently than what people expect. We are learning to love others as God loves them. As we surrender to God's will and move deeper into our belovedness in Christ, God shapes our hearts to truly love people and care for their best interests. We are following Jesus in the cruciform way so we can learn from him how to relate to God and others. Consider Paul's instruction from Philippians 2:3–8:

Do nothing out of selfish ambition or vain conceit. Rather, in humility value others above yourselves, not looking to your own interests but each of you to the interests of the others.

In your relationships with one another, have the same mindset as Christ Jesus:

> Who, being in very nature God,
>> did not consider equality with God something to
>>> be used to his own advantage;
> rather, he made himself nothing
>> by taking the very nature of a servant,
>> being made in human likeness.
> And being found in appearance as a man,
>> he humbled himself
>> by becoming obedient to death—
>>> even death on a cross!

Notice how the mind of Christ is obedient to God *and* looks to the interests or needs of others. Paul says that this mind is yours in Christ Jesus (1 Cor. 2:16). This mind changes us to the very core so that we naturally start to love others from the heart. We care for their needs as much as we care for our own needs—sometimes even more.

This doesn't mean we fall back into the people-pleasing neglect of self-care that leads to burnout. No, we still engage in regular practices that recharge our souls. However, we are now in such a healthy place that *occasionally* we can carefully set aside our needs so that we can minister to others. While we may suffer some harmful effects from this, we are able to bounce back more quickly because we have developed practices to recharge our souls. Like Jesus, we can now notice when we need time alone with the Father so that we can minister to others effectively.

In burnout we neglected self-care because we followed the false self. We wanted to succeed, to receive praise, or to be seen as busy and strong. Now those things don't motivate us as much. Doing God's will is more important, and we know that our self-care and time alone with God are what allow us to hear God's will clearly. Because of this, we are far less likely to burn out. If we are truly living in God's love and surrendered to God's will so that ministry naturally flows from our hearts, burnout is almost impossible.

As we grow in this phase of the journey, the discipline of surrendering to God's will gradually merges with the love of God flowing naturally from our hearts. We have reached full surrender when self-sacrificial love becomes natural to us; then we are living the Spirit-led life.

LIFE OF LOVE

As we grow into God's love and acceptance, we increasingly live a life of *easy obedience*. Love, joy, peace, patience, kindness, goodness, faithfulness, gentleness, and self-control become our identifying traits. The fruit of the Spirit flows naturally from within us. We have learned to abide in Jesus, so the fruit that comes from him shows up in our lives. This does not mean that we have attained sinless perfection. No, we are still aware of our sinfulness, and our false self still pops up from time to time. However, these things no longer characterize or bother us. We now live as someone accepted by God in Christ—a true, Spirit-led self.

Surrender and sacrifice no longer register as emotionally painful like they once did. Instead, we are pulled forward by the internal principle of love, so surrender and sacrifice are joyful. In the same way that Christ endured the cross, we sacrifice because of the joy set before us (Heb. 12:2). This is one of the ways we are better after burnout: we give sacrificially without becoming bitter. This journey from the dessert to the shore makes us resilient and loving. We have a deep, abiding calm rooted in our security in Christ. We respond with patience and empathy instead of frustration. God's faithful covenant love allows him to be long-suffering. This love is now active in us, giving us this freedom too.

As we grow in God's love for us, we become detached from possessions, people, and stress. We begin to live as truly differentiated people. We hold our possessions with open hands. Expecting nothing in return, we lend to others (Luke 6:35). We are even able to hold our closest loved ones in open hands, recognizing that they belong not to us but to God. If God should call them to service that takes them away from us or call us to leave them, we are able to accept this with joy through lament. While we still experience stress and anxiety, they no longer own us. We can step back and put them in perspective because we are led by love. Whatever God asks, we are content with his will. It doesn't matter if we lead or follow because it is our joy to trust the God who is love.

Don't rely on your own work to make spiritual maturity happen. Trust the Spirit to do his work; nothing is impossible for him. If you continue praying for a heart fully surrendered to God's will, the changes described in these chapters will happen in you. You will have the character of Christ in increasing measure. Growth isn't about arriving at perfection; it's about moving closer to Christ.

FREED TO LOVE LIFE

One of the great joys of the life of love is that it frees us to love life again. We are free to move into the world playfully. Not having to prove ourselves to anyone, we can enjoy each moment. Being present allows us to see the wondrous nature of the world. We start to see beauty in so many little things we were too busy to see before. Now we can live an unhurried life because we are following an unhurried God. Moving slowly through the world gives us time to pause and appreciate the beauty of God in all things.

So now you have a choice. You can continue in the frantic, driven life that led to your burnout; you can treat the symptoms of burnout and survive a little longer. Or you can surrender to God and find the freedom to live from love.

1. Meditate on the Colossians 1:9–14. How do you see Paul's prayers being fulfilled in you?
2. How is God working in your life to make you more resilient?
3. What evidence do you see that the love of God is starting to flow from your heart?
4. What would it look like to live fully in God's acceptance of you in Christ? How would your view of yourself change? How would it change how you live toward others?
5. As you think about Jesus's call to the rich young ruler. How does "follow me" sound like an impossible task to you? What works of growth do you need to trust the Holy Spirit for in this season?

16

BEYOND BURNOUT

How long will it take to recover from burnout? This is what most burned-out leaders ask, but they rarely ask the more important question: "How will I know when I am healthy again?" Throughout this book, I've given you a look at what burnout is, practical steps to recover from it, and the spiritual journey to becoming burnout-proof. I want to conclude by painting a picture of a recovered, healthy leader. In chapter 1 I defined burnout as the condition of having your personal identity overwhelmed by the anxiety of life; it's when your inner life with God is no longer able to sustain your outer work for God. *Recovery is when your whole life proceeds from your relationship with God—when the love of God flows naturally from your heart.* As Henri Nouwen said,

> God doesn't burn out. Exhaustion, burnout, and depression are not signs that you are doing God's will. God is gentle and loving. God desires to give you a deep sense of safety in God's love. Once you have allowed yourself to experience that love fully,

you will be better able to discern who you are being sent to in God's name.[1]

In recovery, life is no longer doing things for God or for yourself or for others. *The focus is not on what you are doing but on who you are becoming in God's presence.* Being comes before doing. Recovery is being who God has made you to be: a unified soul with a heart of divine love. We then step out into the world and do what comes from this new heart. In full surrender to God's will, we rediscover our divine design as people made to bear the image of God to the world. As we dwell in God's presence and walk with Jesus, the Holy Spirit reshapes us to be like Jesus. We take on his character and begin to love as he loves. The more we grow into the likeness of Christ, the more we naturally express love, joy, peace, patience, kindness, goodness, faithfulness, gentleness, and self-control. Healthy leadership flows from a heart transformed by the presence of God. That's what recovery looks like.

What we choose to do must flow out of who we are becoming, or we will end up in burnout again. If what we do conflicts with who we are, or if it limits our true self from emerging, we will experience anxiety and internal turmoil. However, if we live from our true self—our Spirit-led self—what we do will express who we are, and no matter what type of work we choose, our leadership will have integrity and purpose.

What does this look like from a practical standpoint? I hesitate to share specifics because, if you're anything like me, you may be tempted to try generating traits artificially instead of first letting them grow in you to become part of your natural being. Please try to resist this temptation. Return to God and let him heal you and transform your heart first. You will know you are healthy when, ruled by love, you are real, connected, purposeful, brave, and gracious.

THE HEALTHY CHRISTIAN LEADER

As I describe the characteristics of a healthy Christian leader, please remember that this is all within the context of being surrendered to God's will and being filled with God's love. Without this reality, Christian leadership is impossible. In fact, Christian leadership that doesn't come from surrender and love is dangerous and destructive. It will only serve to prop up the false self, and it will use people as objects instead of honoring them as individuals who are made to bear God's image. Think of Jesus washing the disciples' feet as the perfect illustration of each of these characteristics. You may want to pause here and meditate on John 13:1–17 before continuing.

Real

A healthy Christian leader is someone who lives life as a unified self. They are the same in every sphere of life: at home, at work, at church, in the community, and in private. What you see is what you get. They have true humility, which should not be confused with self-deprecation or low self-esteem. True humility is knowing exactly who you are. Steve Cuss calls it being exactly human-sized.[2] The healthy Christian leader lives from their true self, the Spirit-led self. They know their strengths, their gifts, and their talents. Leading from these areas allows them to be accepting of their weaknesses. They don't have to be good at everything or present a perfect image to the world. Instead, they are comfortable with their brokenness and limitations. They live each day dependent on God's grace and rooted in God's love. They know where the gaps are in their leadership, and they seek out and accept help from others who can fill those gaps.

The real leader is one who takes time to identify and heal their false self. They are aware of their tendency to project a facade. Instead, they bravely choose to be raw, open, and vulnerable. These leaders have security in Christ so they can face criticism and disagreement with compassion, curiosity, and grace. They are genuinely interested in how others experience them, and they work to dismantle any personal tendencies that get in the way of genuine relationship. These are people with emotional health and emotional intelligence. They are doing the hard work of confronting their resistance and healing their wounds in God's presence.

Healthy leaders also create a safe environment for others to be their authentic selves with them. They do not try to control but allow others to determine their own path. They respect boundaries and do not take responsibility for things that are not theirs to carry. They trust the Holy Spirit to do his work in his time. These leaders are not in a hurry but live in the present moment. They put people ahead of tasks. Real leaders bear the burdens, faults, weaknesses, and brokenness of others because they know their own failings. This allows them to create genuine connection with people. A real leader isn't presenting a manufactured persona or false vulnerability to the world. That's not the type of connection they want. They recognize that true connection with others requires that they present their true, authentic, and vulnerable self.

Connected

A healthy leader is connected to others. Isolation is no longer acceptable for them. First, they are connected to God—Father, Son, and Holy Spirit. They recognize that if they are not in loving relationship with God, they cannot truly love others. They know that their priority is to love God with all their heart, soul, mind, and strength. They also know that they cannot love God until they first receive and apply God's love personally: "We love because he first loved us" (1 John 4:19). Everything they are and everything they do comes from this relationship of love.

Healthy Christian leaders abide in Christ, drawing their life from him because they are united to him. They see Jesus living in intimacy with the Father so that he is nourished by doing the

Father's will and speaking the Father's words.[3] In the same way, healthy leaders approach prayer as listening to God first to know his will. They are energized by their relationship with God. They watch Jesus and learn from him as they read the Scriptures. They don't just find Jesus in the Gospels but have trained their eyes to see him throughout the Bible.

Healthy Christian leaders have a well-developed relationship with the Holy Spirit, and they let the Spirit do his work in his time. They trust that the Spirit is always working and shaping them into the image of Christ. These leaders have an ability to distinguish the voice of the Spirit from their own thoughts and from other voices. They are always listening for the Spirit to speak into their lives through God's Word, other people, and creation (including their new heart). They use this skill to help others discern what the Spirit may be speaking into their lives too.

Healthy leaders are connected to a community. They have a team of people they rely on to help them grow and heal. They aren't afraid to see a counselor, spiritual director, or coach because they know this is not a sign of weakness but of strength. They regularly trust these trained professionals to help them work toward health and wholeness. Healthy leaders also have good friends who love them for who they are and enjoy spending time together. And they are energized and recharged by soul friends with whom they mutually share in the love of God.

Healthy leaders invest in the health of others. They lead from their wounds and heal as they have been healed. They are willing to serve, and their leadership is not controlling but empowering. They are quick to praise and encourage others but are not afraid to speak the hard truths that people need to hear. However, when they say hard things, they say them in love, with gentleness and compassion. Even when they confront others, it's for that person's good and well-being.

This does not mean a healthy leader always has a lot of connections.

They might if they are an extrovert. However, if they are an introvert, they will likely have fewer relationships. The quality of their connections, whether many or few, is the measure of a healthy leader. A leader isn't worried about how many people they know but how they share God's love in the present moment.

Purposeful

Healthy Christian leaders have a clear sense of calling or purpose that is rooted in God's will, which they discern through Scripture and prayer. They also find purpose in their unique gifts, talents, and strengths. Although they seek wisdom from others, they don't let others dictate who they should be. They have already worked to discover how God created them and have a clear vision for their life and leadership. That vision isn't a product of their own intelligence, dreams, or goals. Instead, it develops naturally from their relationship with God as they encounter his will, his design, and his heart. The purpose of a Christian leader will always be empowered by love for others rather than by a desire to prove, earn, or accomplish. This purpose or vision will be held loosely as the leader continually takes time to seek direction from God.

A healthy leader will also have clear values, priorities, and boundaries that keep them on mission. They will not allow peer pressure, amazing opportunities, or self-will to distract them from God's purpose. To ensure they are discerning God's will clearly, they will have a community of discernment around them consisting of godly Christians who are also seeking God first. As this group seeks God in prayer, they develop confidence in God's will, which gives them courage to be brave leaders.

Brave

Secure in God's love for them in Jesus, healthy Christian leaders have a nonanxious presence in their leadership. They remain calm in the face of stress, conflict, and loss because they trust that

God is in control (so they don't have to be). These leaders have the courage to face their fears, their wounds, and their own sinfulness. They bring these to God in lament, confession, and repentance. They know they can't heal themselves, so they enter God's healing presence with raw honesty. They have another Christian or a small group who hears their confession and reminds them of God's love and forgiveness. This allows them to hear criticism with grace and to silence their own inner critic with the love of God and his promises for them in Jesus.

Secure leaders demonstrate health by taking faith-measured risks and not fearing failure. Like Gideon, they see the odds but follow God anyway. When they succeed, they are quick to recognize that God deserves the credit. When they fail, they trust that God is using the experience to help them grow. A brave, healthy leader recognizes that everything is a gift when seen through the lens of God's love and care. This doesn't mean that they welcome tragedy or loss but that they are willing to lament to God without fear. Even when they don't understand what is happening, they hold on to God in faith because they trust in the character and love of the Father. This gives them the freedom to be gracious toward others.

Gracious

Healthy Christian leaders will embody the grace of God in their dealings with others. They will be people of peace, not avoiding conflict but working through conflict toward unity. They will be people who look for outcasts, such as the poor or wounded, people excluded based on their race, gender, education, or country of origin, and even people who have self-excluded. Like Jesus with Zacchaeus, the woman at the well, or the Roman centurion,[4] a healthy leader will pay special attention to those who are on the margins of society (or their organization). These leaders will not simply judge another person because of their situation; instead, they will listen and respond to what the person really needs.

Healthy leaders are quick to forgive and to ask for forgiveness. They keep short accounts and, so far as it depends on them, do not let divisions continue between themselves and others. When they forgive, they truly set the other person free. Though there may still be consequences for wrong actions, their goal is to restore rather than punish the offender. When asking for forgiveness, they own their guilt. They don't blame-shift or turn their apology into a hypothetical (e.g., "I'm sorry if I . . .). Instead, they acknowledge the pain they have caused, show their genuine remorse, and do everything they can to right the wrong.[5] In all things, healthy Christian leaders will show the love, grace, and mercy of God because they themselves are recipients of those blessings.

HEALTH IS A JOURNEY

I wish I could say that I perfectly model real, connected, purposeful, brave, and gracious leadership. This is who I want to be, but I have not yet arrived. *Recovery and health are a direction rather than a destination.* We are all continually on a journey toward greater health. Remember, the faith stages are a series of cycles of growth, not a linear path. Today I am more like the healthy leader I described above than I was a few years ago. As I continue that trend, I am moving toward greater Christlikeness. We are on a journey of becoming. We walk with Jesus and let the Holy Spirit shape us as we become who we were created to be. Rather than looking at the picture of a healthy leader and despairing over how far we must go, we can see who we are becoming. And that image should look like Jesus: humble, real, kind, brave, secure, clear, merciful, loving, and much, much more. Returning to the question from the beginning of this chapter, "What will I look like when I am recovering from burnout and I am becoming healthy?" You will look like a person who is actively becoming more like Jesus.

Your ministry or work will flow increasingly from your relationship with God, the Father.

The final question we need to address is "How can we stay on this journey of becoming like Jesus?" Toward the end of his famous Sermon on the Mount, Jesus said, "Enter through the narrow gate. For wide is the gate and broad is the road that leads to destruction, and many enter through it. But small is the gate and narrow the road that leads to life, and only a few find it" (Matt. 7:13–14). Jesus describes himself as both the gate and the way. He says that following him is the way to life, but this way is difficult and is rarely followed. What can we do to ensure we stay on this narrow road?

Staying on the narrow road isn't easy, and it doesn't come naturally. D. A. Carson describes this difficulty:

> People do not drift toward Holiness. Apart from grace-driven effort, people do not gravitate toward godliness, prayer, obedience to Scripture, faith, and delight in the Lord. We drift toward compromise and call it tolerance; we drift toward disobedience and call it freedom; we drift toward superstition and call it faith. We cherish the indiscipline of lost self-control and call it relaxation; we slouch toward prayerlessness and delude ourselves into thinking we have escaped legalism; we slide toward godlessness and convince ourselves we have been liberated.[6]

Grace-driven effort can be easily mistaken for earning God's favor. I don't think that is what Carson is saying, but if we're not careful, we can tend toward legalism instead of a grace-filled life. The narrow road has ditches on either side. On the left, we can slide away from Christ through spiritual neglect and passivity. On the right, our hyperreligiosity pulls us from Christ through legalistic rules and self-effort. We need a guide to help us avoid the ditches on either side. We need a rule of life.

RULE OF LIFE

As an amateur carpenter, I've built bookcases, kitchen cabinets, and other types of furniture. I enjoy woodworking. The most useful tool in my shop is a four-foot metal ruler that I use to draw straight lines and test my boards to ensure they are flat and true. Without this tool, I wouldn't be able to make good furniture. We all need a good straight edge in life—something to keep us on track and to help us know when things are getting out of true. A rule of life can be just the tool.

Please don't confuse the phrase "rule of life" with "legalistic rules." They are not the same thing. Legalistic rules are put in place to judge whether you have earned your salvation. They are the way judgmental people determine who is in and who is out of the king-dom. The apostle Paul refers to legalistic rules as a false gospel or a distortion of the gospel (see the book of Galatians).

A rule of life is not about earning or determining salvation. Rather, it's a clear picture of what we need to live in healthy relation-ship with God. It's a collection of individually tailored spiritual practices that help us focus our attention on God. We insert these practices into our daily, weekly, monthly, and yearly rhythms to help us remain on the narrow road. A rule of life might also be called rhythms for life. Your rule of life will be a way to bring everything you've learned in this book into a single plan for continued growth and resilience.

The idea of a rule of life comes from Saint Benedict, a sixth-century Catholic monk who wrote "A Little Rule for Beginners." There are many ways to form a rule of life, and Benedict's guide is helpful. Stephen A. Macchia wrote an excellent book called *Crafting a Rule of Life: An Invitation to the Well-Ordered Way*. He offers twelve steps or lessons as a modern interpretation of Benedict's rule. If you want to dig deeply into creating your own rule of life, I highly recommend this resource. You can find a simple summary of how to develop this practice in appendix 2, "How to Create a Rule of Life."

BETTER AFTER BROKEN

Your burnout doesn't have to be an ending. I believe with the right focus, some hard work, and a community of helpful people around you, this time in your life could be a catalyst that God uses to initiate growth. Recovering from burnout will make you a more Christlike leader in the long run. Your burnout is now part of your story, but it doesn't have to define you. God can use it to create something beautiful. In time, I believe you will see your burnout as a gift from God.

The Japanese have an artistic and spiritual practice called *kintsugi*. *Kintsugi* means "to mend with gold" (*kin* means "gold," and *tsugi* means "to mend"). A kintsugi master would behold the fragments of a broken bowl for a long time before mending it, rejoining broken pieces of pottery using lacquer and gold.[7] They have a philosophy or spirituality that embraces the broken or flawed as something that is beautiful in its own way. "The brokenness is part of the object's story but not the end of that story. *Kintsugi* transforms a normal piece of pottery into a functional work of art. In many ways, Jesus does the same for us. He takes our brokenness and makes it beautiful."[8]

In the same way, your burnout is something God will make beautiful if you are willing to let his Spirit do the work of rebuilding your soul. As you work through recovery and build your spiritual life on God's love for you in Christ, you will become a stronger and better leader than you ever could have been before burnout. Without this trial by fire, you never would have melted off the dross that was holding you back. You would still be living from your false self. Now you can become real, connected, purposeful, brave, and gracious because you are rooted and grounded in God's love.

Remember, healthy recovery is a journey, not a destination. I invite you to join Jesus by walking the narrow road that leads to life. I hope to see you along that road. Maybe the Spirit will let us travel together for a time.

1. Imagine yourself as a real, connected, purposeful, brave, and gracious leader. What excites you about this idea?
2. As you start your journey toward resilience and recovery, where are you now and where are you going (your personal goal)?
3. What are the first few steps for you on this journey?
4. Read the second appendix, "How to Create a Rule of Life." How would developing a rule of life help you synthesize the concepts in this book?
5. How can you help other leaders with what you've learned in this book?

APPENDIX 1

PLANNING YOUR SABBATH

Jewish families often use rituals to help them plan and prepare for the Sabbath. This guide is designed to help you discover your own rituals to make your Sabbath day the most life-giving day of the week. As you make the following lists, think about what leads you to wonder, worship, gratitude, laughter, and contentment. Approach your Sabbath playfully, not as a religious duty but as a gift from God for your own refreshment.

1. List some people who give life to your soul, people who love and appreciate you for who you are and not necessarily for what you do, people whose company you truly enjoy and who enjoy yours, people who do not drain your soul.
2. List some physical locations that help you be more aware of God's presence. These may be places of beauty, places associated with special memories, or new places you feel led to explore. If there is a cost involved with visiting these places, be sure to note that too.

3. List your favorite foods or drinks that bring joy to your soul or cause you to give thanks to God. (This principle comes from Deuteronomy 14:26.)

4. List some music that helps you worship God, that brings peace to your heart, or that makes you happy. (If it makes you want to dance, even better!)

5. List some playful activities. These are things you enjoy doing for the mere pleasure of doing them (e.g., games, sports, hobbies, dance, theater, movies).

6. List some restful activities that restore your spirit (e.g., naps, meditation, reading, journaling, mindfulness practices).

7. List some things that help you notice God's presence or that are beautiful to you (e.g., candles, campfires, scents, art, poetry).

8. List some spiritual disciplines that are meaningful to you or that you would like to try.

DEVELOP A SABBATH PLAN

Prayerfully look over your Sabbath lists. The following questions might be helpful in planning your next Sabbath day:

1. When will you practice your Sabbath? Decide what time this week you will set aside as your Sabbath. Set aside a full twenty-four-hour period, preferably starting before sundown (e.g., 7:00 p.m. Saturday to 7:00 p.m. Sunday). Try to include the whole family so you can all enjoy the same Sabbath day together. Plan your Sabbath for the same time every week.

2. What spiritual activities will you do to connect with God

and to be more aware of his presence (e.g., worship, Bible reading, prayer, spiritual disciplines)? Be sure to plan these first as they are most important to the practice of Sabbath.

3. What activities that bring joy to your soul do you feel led to include?

4. Plan a special meal with family or friends. This is a great way to start your Sabbath.

5. What items of beauty will you use throughout your day to remind you of God's presence?

6. Be sure to leave open spaces in your Sabbath day for silence, solitude, physical rest, or spontaneous fun.

7. Decide what ritual you will use to signal the ending of the Sabbath.

8. Schedule a time for planning next week's Sabbath.

THINGS TO AVOID ON THE SABBATH

The Sabbath is about ceasing from our productivity and receiving God's love and good gifts. So it's helpful to disconnect from the following things in order to focus on God:

- Work
- Electronic media (email, social media, TV)
- Productivity
- Attempts to control
- Perfection
- Aggressive activity
- Power
- Planning
- Judgment

THINGS THAT MIGHT SURFACE AS YOUR SOUL BEGINS TO REST

As you spend time away from the busyness and productivity of life, fewer things can distract you from what is happening in your soul. This is good because it allows the hidden, wounded, or unwanted parts of you to come into God's presence for healing. As you notice these things, name them in God's presence. Be honest about them, express them as fully as you can, and then move on. Try to avoid judging yourself or your feelings. Here is what might surface in your soul:

- Anger
- Anxiety
- Fear
- Sadness
- Grief
- Sorrow
- Aggression
- Sin

ATTITUDES TO ADOPT ON THE SABBATH

The Sabbath is a good time to reflect on what Jesus values and how he expressed his character. Intentionally, choose and adopt those same values on the Sabbath. You will soon find them showing up on the other days too. Here's a partial list:

- Love
- Joy
- Peace
- Patience
- Kindness
- Goodness
- Faithfulness
- Gentleness
- Self-Control
- Thankfulness
- Playfulness
- Grace and Mercy
- Forgiveness
- Truthfulness
- Authenticity

RESOURCES FOR SABBATH PLANNING

Sabbath: The Ancient Practices by Dan Allender

Sacred Rhythms by Ruth Haley Barton

Strengthening the Soul of Your Leadership by Ruth Haley Barton

Sabbath as Resistance by Walter Brueggemann

Keeping the Sabbath Wholly: Ceasing, Resting, Embracing, Feasting by Marva J. Dawn

Unhurried Living by Alan Fadling

The Unhurried Leader by Alan Fadling

The Sabbath by Abraham Joshua Heschel

Rhythms of Rest: Finding the Spirit of Sabbath in a Busy World by Shelly Miller

Sabbath: Finding Rest, Renewal, and Delight in Our Busy Lives by Wayne Muller

Emotionally Healthy Spirituality by Pete Scazzero

The Emotionally Healthy Leader by Pete Scazzero

Subversive Sabbath by A. J. Swoboda

APPENDIX 2

HOW TO CREATE A RULE OF LIFE

To create your own rule of life you will need to have clarity on your core values, your priorities, and your boundaries. You'll also need to know your life rhythms, gifts, talents, and personality. As you craft a rule of life, you will be bringing all these things under the rule of God and surrendering them to his will. If you have already done this work, you are ready to begin forming your rule.

PRAY AND LISTEN

Hopefully by now you are learning that all Christian leadership starts with prayer and listening to the voice of God. Discerning your rule of life is no different. We need to start by becoming aware of God's presence and being silent before him. As we sit in silence, we are to listen to the Spirit and the Word for direction from God. For each of the subsequent steps, let the Holy Spirit guide your decisions.

NOTICE YOUR LIFE RHYTHMS

Take some time to notice and evaluate your life rhythms. What rhythms of work and rest do you currently observe? Include your patterns for sleep, work, exercise, and eating. While this isn't an exercise in time management, our weekly calendars can be useful at this point. In discerning our life rhythms, we must notice the ebb and flow of our physical, spiritual, mental, and emotional energies as they relate to the calendar. For example, what times of the day and week do you feel most physically energized? When does your body most often feel fatigued? Chart your emotional, mental, and spiritual vitality too. When do you feel closest to God? When does he feel most distant? Benedict called these *consolations* and *desolations*.

Think through your daily, weekly, monthly, and yearly rhythms. When do you feel high or low energy? Try to understand *why* you feel this way. What patterns do you see emerging? Be careful to also notice when you are getting healthy rest and nutrition and when you are deprived or taking in too much. How do these patterns affect you?

As you notice your healthy and unhealthy life rhythms, try to evaluate them objectively. It usually helps to write them down or create a chart so that you can step back and see the big picture. You might need help from a friend or professional to ensure you are seeing yourself clearly.

Now ask yourself these questions:

- Where do I need to be closer to God in my day, week, month, or year? This may mean you are more aware of his presence or more filled with his love or more discerning of his will. Where do you need to see God more in your rhythms?
- Where do I need to make changes to be the most healthy version of myself? These changes can be physical, mental, emotional, social, or spiritual. Examine your health in each area.

- Where in my calendar do I see conflicts between my false self and my true self? What needs to change in order to become more wholehearted?

IDENTIFY SPIRITUAL PRACTICES

Now identify some spiritual practices that help you connect with God on a deeper level. Look at the spiritual practices covered in chapter 10 and in the workbook.[1] Try several of these practices on for size. Which ones are most helpful for you? Which ones do nothing for you? Try to identify a few spiritual practices that will enhance your times of Bible reading, prayer, corporate worship, and Sabbath. What other spiritual practices would be helpful throughout other parts of the week? A spiritual director can be immensely helpful during this phase.

INCORPORATE SPIRITUAL PRACTICES WITHIN YOUR RHYTHMS

Now you are ready to write your rule of life. Here you are going to incorporate your chosen spiritual practices and healthy lifestyle changes into your regular life rhythms. It's okay to have a plan, but start small. Pick the easiest spiritual practice and healthy habit to adopt. Do those until they feel natural before incorporating more changes.

> **DAILY:** Break up your day into four to six equal sections (early morning, late morning, early afternoon, late afternoon, evening, and bedtime). What spiritual practices or healthy habits feel right for each time?
>
> **WEEKLY:** What weekly rhythms will you need to incorporate or improve? If you aren't practicing a weekly Sabbath or weekly corporate worship, these are a good place to start.

MONTHLY: Are there monthly practices that would help you in your relationship with God? I find it helpful to take one day per month as a mini prayer retreat. This also gives me space to lament, grieve, or give healthy expression to any emotions I was tempted to bury.

YEARLY: Are there patterns in your year where you need extra rest or deeper connection with God? What are your most draining times of the year? Plan time before and after to energize your body, mind, and soul. Seasonal vacations or extended prayer retreats can be helpful here. You would be wise to incorporate a sabbatical every five to seven years for renewal and realignment.

Now that you've created a plan by incorporating new spiritual practices and healthy habits into your life rhythms, build the rest of your life around them. Let your relationship with God and the care of your soul form the basis for the rest of your life and work.

ADJUST YOUR RULE AS NEEDED

As you start to live this new rule of life, you may find that your relationships are affected by it. In some cases this will be a good change. However, if you see it having negative effects on your most important relationships, renegotiate your rule. The goal is for your rule of life to *enhance* your relationship with God and your love for others. If your rule gets in the way of loving God or loving others, then it is not a healthy rule of life.

You may also find that over time certain spiritual practices lose their effectiveness. This is normal. It may mean you have drifted out of focus and aren't really giving yourself to the practices. If that's the case, try to reengage. However, you may need to mix things up and try a different practice or adjust your rhythms. Don't get so locked into your rule of life that it feels like a burden. It is supposed to unlock your freedom and joy, so approach it playfully. Like a child on the playground, feel free to change the rules to make the "game" more life-giving.

.

ACKNOWLEDGMENTS

There aren't enough pages to express the depth of gratitude I feel toward so many who helped make this book possible. Please accept these few words as a single drop of the flood of thanks you all deserve.

To my family—

- Amy, my wife, my editor, my best friend, you inspire me to be a better man and a better writer. The way you craft language into meaning and beauty will always astound me. Most of all, your love for Christ teaches me every day. I could not have survived these difficult years without your example, your support, and your grace. I believe our best years are ahead because I see more of Jesus in you every day.
- Ben, my son, I am so proud of the man you have become. I'm sorry so many of your formative years were when you had a burned-out dad. I hope that you were still able to see my joy in you. I love laughing with you. Keep seeking Jesus because he is of more value than this whole world.
- Mom and Dad, I am blessed by your love and support. I couldn't have written this book if it weren't for the stable foundation of faith and hope in Christ that you formed in me.

- Mike and Josh, your love for me kept me going through some of my darkest times. I was strong because I didn't want to let my little brothers down. I admire you both so much.

To the people of FBC—For eighteen years you loved me and my family despite my mistakes and struggles. As I look back on our time together, I wish I had spent less time focused on what I thought needed to change and more time dwelling on the good and wonderful things that God was doing among us.

To my soul friends and listening group—Byard, Shalini, Jack, Sharon, Su, Don, Nathan, Sandra, Shelly, and Renny: you accepted me for who I am, and that is a rare gift. From you, I learned just how desperately my soul longed for true friendship. You all were like an oasis in the desert, and I hope I am always able to drink deeply of your friendship and love in Christ.

To my burnout recovery team—Friend Jessie, Pastor Dave, Counselor Nate, Coach Dave, and Spiritual Director Josh: you each offered friendship, pastoral help, and expertise in my darkest moments. You became the lifeline that saved me from drowning.

To the pastors I've coached—I hope I have given you half as much as what you have taught me. You welcomed me into your life with fearless trust and showed me what courageous healing looks like. It has been my honor to walk with you in your journey as you did the hard work. Thank you for enduring my probing questions with honesty and grace. I am amazed at what the Holy Spirit is doing in you all.

To the team at PIR Ministries—Roy, Tom, Jason, Dan, Cal, Robin, and others: it is an honor to serve pastors and their families alongside you. It's been so good for me to be part of a team that collaborates, challenges one another, and so deeply appreciates each other.

To my Soul Care Institute Cohort 7 family—Skeet, Angie, Katy, Joe, Steve, Gwen, Chuck, Fil, Tara, Howard, Doug, Adele, Kaylene,

Jimm, and others. When I met you, I knew that I had found my people. Your welcoming spirit, open hearts, and love for Christ made you a safe tribe where I could heal and grow. Continue to trust in the slow work of God.

To the authors who inspire me most—Sharon Garlough Brown, Steve Cuss, Chuck DeGroat, Charles Stone, and Karl Vaters. Your influence and writings are all over this book. You each write books that make me want to write to help others. Your wisdom, encouragement, and support have meant the world to me. Thank you for enduring my questions about writing, publishing, and promotion. Most of all, thank you for being so eager to read and endorse this book so that others could have confidence in a previously unpublished author.

To my early readers, most of whom are mentioned in other sections, plus Darrell, Jodie, Mary, JoLynn, and Tim—thank you for enduring my unedited mess. You helped me understand what was working and what needed to be fixed. You made this book so much better!

To the Zondervan Reflective team—Alexis, thank you for believing in this project and coaching me to write a better book proposal. Kyle, your skill as a writer and editor improved this book greatly. Your passion for helping pastors is inspiring. Kara, your suggestions were so helpful! The rest of the team, including Matt Estel, Sheryl Moon, and others, thank you for your work behind the scenes handling every detail in the book-making process. This book wouldn't be possible without you!

Lord Jesus, thank you for the gift of every person listed above, for your love and grace, and most of all for giving yourself that I might be yours. Please, use this book to help others find themselves in you.

NOTES

Introduction

1. The stories and examples in this book are based on real-life examples. The names and a detail or two may have been changed to protect the anonymity of the subjects. In a couple of cases, two stories were blended into one illustration.

Chapter 1: Am I in Burnout?

1. David Dekok, *Fire Underground: The Ongoing Tragedy of the Centralia Mine Fire* (Guilford, CT: Rowman & Littlefield, 2009), 21.

2. Mayo Clinic Staff, "Job Burnout: How to Spot It and Take Action," Mayo Clinic, June 5, 2021, https://www.mayoclinic.org/healthy -lifestyle/adult-health/in-depth/burnout/art-20046642.

3. "Burn-Out and 'Occupational Phenomenon': International Classification of Diseases," World Health Organization, May 28, 2019, https://www.who.int/news/item/28-05-2019-burn-out-an -occupational-phenomenon-international-classification-of-diseases.

4. Henri Nouwen, *In the Name of Jesus* (New York: Crossroad, 1992), 21.

5. Leslie J. Francis, Patrick Laycock, and Henry Ratter, "Testing the Francis Burnout Inventory among Anglican clergy in England," *Mental Health, Religion, and Culture* 22, no. 10 (2019):1057–67.

6. Christina Maslach et al., "Maslach Burnout Toolkit for General Use,"

Mind Garden, 2016, https://www.mindgarden.com/332-maslach
-burnout-toolkit-for-general-use.

7. The Maslach Burnout Inventory identifies three areas for diagnosing
   burnout: (1) emotional exhaustion, (2) depersonalization or cynicism,
   and (3) professional efficacy. I have separated elements of the
   depersonalization into "loss of self" and "hopelessness" because these
   terms have proven to be clearer for the pastors I coach.

8. Merriam-Webster.com, s.v. "Compassion fatigue," https://www
   .merriam-webster.com/dictionary/compassion%20fatigue.

9. Wes Beavis, *Let's Talk about Ministry Burnout: A Proven Research-Based
   Approach to the Wellbeing of Pastors* (Newport Beach, CA: Wesley James
   Beavis, PsyD / Powerborn, 2019), 1–2. This book is only available at
   www.DrWesBeavis.com.

10. Rose Zimering and Suzy Bird Gulliver, "Secondary Traumatization
    in Mental Health Care Providers," *Psychiatric Times* 20, no. 4 (2003),
    https://www.psychiatrictimes.com/view/secondary-traumatization
    -mental-health-care-providers.

11. I've dropped the word *disorder* after *posttraumatic stress* (PTS) because
    mental health professionals are starting to see that this term brings
    shame and can get in the way of treatment. Additionally, it's not
    really a disorder; it's a natural response to trauma in many but not all
    people. It's not a disorder; it's a trauma response.

12. See https://www.ptsd.va.gov/.

13. Heather Davediuk Gingrich, *Restoring the Shattered Self: A Christian
    Counselor's Guide to Complex Trauma* (Downers Grove, IL: IVP
    Academic, 2013).

14. Wes Beavis, *Let's Talk about Ministry Burnout*, 12–13.

Chapter 2: Many Paths to Burnout

1. "PRO-D Assessment," PIR Ministries, https://pirministries.org
   /ministries/pro-d-professional-development/.

Chapter 3: The Inner Life

1. Sarah Pruitt, "5 Things You Might Not Know about the Challenger
   Shuttle Disaster," History.com, updated January 25, 2021, https://www

.history.com/news/5-things-you-might-not-know-about-the-challenger
-shuttle-disaster.

2. "Compartmentalization—n. a defense mechanism in which thoughts and feelings that seem to conflict or to be incompatible are isolated from each other in separate and apparently impermeable psychic compartments." *APA Dictionary of Psychology*, s.v. compartmentalization, https://dictionary.apa.org/compartmentalization.

3. Chuck DeGroat, *Wholeheartedness* (Grand Rapids: Eerdmans, 2016), 5.

4. Merriam-Webster.com, s.v. "disintegrate," https://www.merriam -webster.com/dictionary/disintegrate.

5. DeGroat, *Wholeheartedness*, 72.

6. You may not know both your parents or your grandparents, but their influence may still be present. You may also have adoptive parents who have passed on their family scripts to you, in which case your biological parents would not have much influence.

7. This is a paraphrase of a well-known quote generally attributed to Abigail Van Buren: "The church is a hospital for sinners, not a museum for saints." However, variations of this saying have been attributed to others throughout history going as far back as St. Augustine of Hippo.

8. If you are a pastor in need of help, PIR Ministries stands ready to provide a healing space. Contact us at pirministries.org.

9. DeGroat, *Wholeheartedness*, 60.

Chapter 4: Stress and Burnout

1. Wikipedia, "Tacoma Narrows Bridge (1940)," https://en.wikipedia .org/wiki/Tacoma_Narrows_Bridge_(1940).

2. Wikipedia, "Tacoma Narrows Bridge (1940)."

3. Gina, Francesca, "Are You Too Stressed to Be Productive? Or Not Stressed Enough?," *Harvard Business Review*, April 14, 2016, https:// hbr.org/2016/04/are-you-too-stressed-to-be-productive-or-not -stressed-enough.

4. Steve Cuss, *Managing Leadership Anxiety: Yours and Theirs* (Nashville: Nelson, 2019), 7.

5. The names and events in these case studies are fictitious, but they

have basis in real stories from my own experience and from the lives of leaders I've worked with.

6. Cuss, *Managing Leadership Anxiety*, 18.

7. Curt Thompson, *The Soul of Shame: Retelling the Stories We Believe About Ourselves* (Downers Grove, IL: InterVarsity, 2015), 63.

8. Thompson, *The Soul of Shame*, 31.

Chapter 5: Energy and Rhythms

1. Data on the 2001 earthquake and tsunami come from the following sources: "Tsunami Facts in Wake of Japan Earthquake," *National Geographic*, March 11, 2011, https://www.nationalgeographic.com/science/article/110311-tsunami-facts-japan-earthquake-hawaii; Becky Oskin, "Japan Earthquake and Tsunami of 2011: Facts and Information," Live Science, February 25, 2022, https://www.livescience.com/39110-japan-2011-earthquake-tsunami-facts.html; "How a Tsunami Wave Works," National Oceanography Centre, March 11, 2011, https://noc.ac.uk/news/how-tsunami-wave-works; "Tracking Debris from the Tokoku Tsunami," NASA Earth Observatory, April 3, 2012, https://earthobservatory.nasa.gov/images/77489/tracking-debris-from-the-tohoku-tsunami#.

2. Byung-Chul Han, *The Burnout Society* (Stanford: Stanford University Press, 2015), 22.

3. "Yoke," *Dictionary of Biblical Imagery*, ed. Leland Ryken, James C. Wilhoit, Tremper Longman III (Downers Grove, IL: InterVarsity, 1998), 975.

4. Alan Fadling, *The Unhurried Leader* (Downers Grove, IL: InterVarsity, 2017), 17.

Chapter 6: Reconnecting

1. BUD/S stands for Basic Underwater Demolition/SEAL.

2. I first read this story in Henry Cloud's book *The Power of the Other* (New York: Harper Business, 2016). I've retold the story to fit with the theme of this book, adding details on the nature of SEAL training from the following sources: https://www.sealswcc.com

/navy-seal-swcc-training-pipeline.html; "BUD/S (Basic Underwater Demolition/SEAL) Training," Navy SEALs.com, www.Navyseals .com/nsw/bud-s-basic-underwater-demolition-seal-training/.

3. Cloud, *The Power of the Other*.

4. Learn more about being a nonanxious presence in Alex Friedman's book *Failure of Nerve: Leadership in the Age of the Quick Fix*, 10th anniv. rev. ed. (New York: Church, 2017).

5. Barbara L. Peacock, *Soul Care in African American Practice* (Downers Grove, IL: InterVarsity Press, 2020), Kindle location 100

6. William A. Barry and William J. Connolly, *The Practice of Spiritual Direction* (New York: HarperCollins, 2009), 8.

7. Ruth Haley Barton, "Make a Joyful Silence," Transforming Center, https://transformingcenter.org/2009/02/make-a-joyful-silence/.

8. Henri Nouwen, *Spiritual Direction: Wisdom for the Long Walk of Faith* (New York: HarperCollins, 2006), 19.

9. Peacock, *Soul Care in African American Practice*, chapter 2.

10. John Townsend, *People Fuel* (Grand Rapids: Zondervan, 2019), 81ff. I highly recommend this book for everyone working through burnout.

Chapter 7: Restoration of Self

1. David G. Benner, *The Gift of Being Yourself: The Sacred Call to Self-Discovery* (Downers Grove, IL: InterVarsity Press, 2015), 70.

2. DeGroat, *Wholeheartedness*, 85.

3. According to *The Brown-Driver-Briggs Hebrew and English Lexicon* (2004), *nephesh* can mean (depending on context) soul, living being, life, self, person, desire, appetite, emotion, and passion.

4. John 4:34.

5. John 12:49.

6. John 5:19.

7. Alison Cook and Kimberly Miller, *Boundaries for Your Soul* (Nashville: Nelson, 2018), 26.

8. Cook and Miller curated this list from Richard C. Schwartz, *Introduction to the Internal Family Systems Model* (Oak Park, IL: Trailhead, 2001), 33–48.

Chapter 8: Becoming Secure

1. Marcus Peter Johnson, *One with Christ: An Evangelical Theology of Salvation* (Wheaton, IL: Crossway, 2013), 17–18.

2. Confession and repentance are often confused in the church today. *Confession* is saying what we've done. It literally means "to say the same thing," that is, to agree with God about our sin. *Repentance* is changing one's behavior and going in the opposite direction. We repent when we stop sinning and start living from the love of God within us—loving God and others from the heart.

3. This is not to say that an abused person immediately feels safe around their abuser because they have forgiven them. It means that the abused person no longer has to harbor hate toward their abuser in their heart while maintaining wise boundaries and safe distance.

Chapter 9: Differentiation of Self

1. Charles Stone Jr., *People-Pleasing Pastors: Avoiding the Pitfalls of Approval-Motivated Leadership* (Downers Grove, IL: InterVarsity Press, 2014), 67.

2. Jamey Johnson, "Codependent Pastoral Leadership—It's Exhausting!," JameyJohnsonDotOrg, April 16, 2007, https://jamey jjohnson.typepad.com/my_weblog/2007/04/codependent_pas.html.

3. Rich Villodas (@richvillodas), Twitter, October 6, 2020, 5:27 p.m., https://twitter.com/richvillodas/status/1313591655036071949.

4. Michael Kerr and Murray Bowen, *Family Evaluation: The Role of Family as an Emotional Unit That Governs Individual Behavior and Development* (New York: Norton, 1988), 97–109.

5. Peter L. Steinke, *Congregational Leadership in Anxious Times: Being Calm and Courageous No Matter What* (Lanham, MD: Rowman & Littlefield), Kindle loc. 415–16.

6. Peter Scazzero, *Emotionally Healthy Spirituality* (Grand Rapids: Zondervan, 2017), 82.

7. "Differentiation of Self," The Bowen Center for the Study of the Family, https://www.thebowencenter.org/differentiation-of-self.

8. Charles Stone, *Holy Noticing: The Bible, Your Brain, and the Mindful Space Between Moments* (Chicago: Moody, 2019), 16.

9. Stone, *Holy Noticing*, 33.

10. For a deeper, more thorough mindfulness practice, read *Holy Noticing*.

Chapter 10: Soul Care

1. Download a .pdf of the Sabbath Planning Guide at https://pastorsoul .com/2020/05/11/planning-your-sabbath/.

2. Bivocational pastors often tell me that they can't find one twenty -four-hour period. So I encourage them to find twenty-four hours throughout the week—better to have many little Sabbaths than none at all. Usually, after a few months of this, they find a way to bring their twenty-four hours together into a single Sabbath day.

Chapter 11: Boundaries

1. There's also a list of questions in the *Weary Leader's Guide to Burnout Workbook* available for free download at seannemecek.com/WLGB workbook.

2. Greg McKeown, *Essentialism: The Disciplined Pursuit of Less* (New York: Crown Business, 2014), 16.

3. Henry Cloud and John Townsend, *Boundaries* (Grand Rapids: Zondervan, 1992), 31.

4. Adapted from Cloud and Townsend, *Boundaries*, chapter 5, "Ten Laws of Boundaries."

5. Kabir Sehgal and Deepak Chopra, "Stanford Professor: Working This Many Hours a Week Is Basically Pointless. Here's How to Get More Done—by Doing Less," CNBC, March 20, 2019, https://www.cnbc .com/2019/03/20/stanford-study-longer-hours-doesnt-make-you-more -productive-heres-how-to-get-more-done-by-doing-less.html.

6. Maria Konnikova, "The Limits of Friendship," *The New Yorker*, October 7, 2014, https://www.newyorker.com/science/maria -konnikova/social-media-affect-math-dunbar-number-friendships.

Chapter 12: Breaking Free

1. Scazzero, *Emotionally Healthy Spirituality*, 75.

2. More help in constructing a genogram including a genogram chart and list of symbols is available in the *Weary Leader's Guide to Burnout*

Workbook available for download at seannemecek.com/WLGB workbook.

3. "How to Make a Genogram: 3 Steps," GenoPro, https://genopro.com /articles/how-to-create-a-genogram/.

4. Cuss, *Managing Leadership Anxiety*, 70.

5. Cuss, *Managing Leadership Anxiety*, 75.

Chapter 13: Never Burn Out Again

1. Janet O. Hagberg and Robert A. Guelich, *The Critical Journey: Stages in the Life of Faith* (Salem, WI: Sheffield, 2005), viii.

Chapter 14: Surrender to God

1. Hagberg and Guelich, *Critical Journey*, 115.

2. Ruth Haley Barton, *Strengthening the Soul of Your Leadership: Seeking God in the Crucible of Ministry* (Downers Grove, IL: InterVarsity, 2018), 201–2.

3. C.S. Lewis, *The Last Battle* (London: HarperCollins, 2009), 210.

Chapter 16: Beyond Burnout

1. Henri Nouwen Society, "God Doesn't Get Burned Out" (meditation), July 18, https://henrinouwen.org/meditation/god-doesnt-get-burned -out/.

2. "Managing or Being Managed: Steve Cuss on Leadership Anxiety," *Hope Renewed* (podcast), December 7, 2020, https://anchor.fm/hope -renewed/episodes/Managing-or-Being-Managed-Steve-Cuss-on -Leadership-Anxiety-ena91b.

3. "Jesus said to them, 'My food is to do the will of him who sent me and to accomplish his work'" (John 4:34).

4. See Luke 19:1–10; John 4; and Matthew 8:5–13, respectively.

5. See Zacchaeus's response to Jesus in Luke 19:8.

6. D. A. Carson, *For the Love of God*, vol. 2 (Wheaton, IL: Crossway), Jan. 23.

7. Makoto Fugimura, "Kintsugi Generation," *Makoto Fugimura Writings* (blog), May 5, 2019, https://makotofujimura.com/writings/kintsugi -generation/.

8. Sean Nemecek, "Am I Damaged Goods?," *The Pastor's Soul* (blog), February 19, 2020, https://pastorsoul.com/2020/02/19/am-i-damaged -goods/.

Appendix 2: How to Create a Rule of Life

1. The workbook is downloadable at https://seannemecek.com/WLGB workbook/.